PAINTING THE WILD FRONTIER

PAINTING THE WILD FRONTIER

The Art and Adventures of
George Catlin

SUSANNA REICH

CLARION BOOKS

New York

Clarion Books
a Houghton Mifflin Company imprint
215 Park Avenue South, New York, NY 10003
Copyright © 2008 by Susanna Reich

The text was set in 13-point Sabon.
Book design by Trish Parcell Watts.

www.clarionbooks.com

Printed in China.

Library of Congress Cataloging-in-Publication Data

Reich, Susanna.
Painting the wild frontier : the art and adventures of George Catlin / by Susanna Reich.
p. cm.
Includes bibliographical references and index.
ISBN 978-0-618-71470-4
1. Catlin, George, 1796–1872—Juvenile literature. 2. Painters—United States—Biography—Juvenile literature.
3. Indians in art—Juvenile literature. 4. West (U.S.)—In art—Juvenile literature. I. Title.
ND237.C35R45 2008
759.13—dc22
[B]   2007038847

WKT 10 9 8 7 6 5 4 3 2 1

FRONTISPIECE: *GEORGE CATLIN,* BY R. STANLEY FREEMAN.
PHOTOGRAPH, 1870. VIRGINIA MUSEUM OF FINE ARTS, RICHMOND.
THE PAUL MELLON COLLECTION. © VIRGINIA MUSEUM OF FINE ARTS.

To Matthew Reich,
who has always loved a good adventure

ACKNOWLEDGMENTS

This book is the product of several years of research, during which I received assistance and support from many people. I would like to thank George Gurney, Chief Curator, Smithsonian American Art Museum, and Nancy Anderson, Curator of American and British Paintings, National Gallery of Art, for taking the time to meet with me and answer my questions. Thanks also to Marjorie Catlin Stevenson and Lindsey Stevenson Schlegel, descendants of George Catlin, for allowing me to reproduce George's painting of Putnam Catlin.

For help with images and permissions I am grateful to the following institutions and individuals: Callie Morfeld Vincent, Amon Carter Museum; Wendy Hurlock Baker, Archives of American Art; Annemarie Donahue, Buffalo Bill Historical Center; Yann-Arzel Durelle-Marc, Center of the History of Law, University of Rennes; Erin Tikovitsch, Chicago History Museum; Carole Lee Vowell, Denver Art Museum; Dana Yarbrough and Shane Culpepper, Gilcrease Museum; Nancy Sherbert, Kansas State Historical Society; Julie Frey, The Litchfield Historical Society; Susan Nurse, Memorial Art Gallery of the University of Rochester; Raymond Khan and Dina Selfridge, Mid-Manhattan Library Picture Collection, New York Public Library; Peter Huestis and Barbara Wood, National Gallery of Art; Lizanne Garrett, National Portrait Gallery; Barbara Katus, Pennsylvania Academy of the Fine Arts; Richard H. Sorensen, Smithsonian American Art Museum; Kim Robinson, U.S. Department of the Interior Museum; and Howell W. Perkins, Virginia Museum of Fine Arts.

I would like to thank the staff of the Ossining Public Library, especially John Hawkins, for help with interlibrary loans, and Sally Dow, Judith Sagat, and Marci Dressler for their expertise in children's books and longtime support of my work.

Thanks also to my indefatigable editor, Lynne Polvino, for her patience, intelligence, and enthusiasm; to my art director, Joann Hill, for her keen eye; and to my agent, Tracey Adams, for championing my work. Jim Armstrong provided thoughtful, reassuring, and much-appreciated guidance on the manuscript, and Trish Parcell Watts worked design magic. To my tribe—the authors, artists, and editors of Kindling Words—my gratitude for so openly sharing their wisdom and experience. To my colleagues Susan Raab, Joyce Stein, Tara Koppel, Bobbie Combs, Laurina Cashin, Joan Honig, and Kristen Pisanelli, thanks for generous advice and warm friendship.

Lastly, my grateful thanks to my husband, Gary Golio, and daughter, Laurel Golio, for their patience through many days and nights when I was distracted by work. Laurel's anthropological advice has been invaluable, and she takes terrific pictures, too. Gary is first reader, word guru, and best friend, and this book would not exist without his constant encouragement, deep knowledge of art history, and insight into the human heart.

Contents

Foreword

GEORGE CATLIN (1796–1872) is best known as the premier nineteenth-century painter of Native Americans. Though he studied law as a young man, he became a professional artist, and his most significant contribution was documenting the cultures and lives of Plains Indians. Catlin lived during one of the most complex periods in American history, a time of remarkable advances in the sciences and arts that was also marked by tremendous political change and conflict. It was an age of global expansion and imperialism for the major European powers, and of massive westward expansion of the United States. Spurred on by the concept of Manifest Destiny—the belief that the United States had the God-given right to possess the whole of the North American continent—the government undertook an explicit agenda of expansionism that included annexing huge amounts of territory, building railroads, and attempting to eradicate powerful Indian cultures. It is this context that informed Catlin's work and shaped his ambitions.

From 1831 to 1836, when he was in his mid- to late thirties, George Catlin traveled throughout the American West to paint the Indians, recording not only their faces and dress but also their ceremonies, aspects of their daily lives, and their physical surroundings. He created formal portraits of distinguished Indian leaders and warriors dressed in regalia, as well as groupings of family members and mothers with their children. In other paintings, he documented religious ceremonies and dances, sweeping landscapes, and even buffalo-hunting scenes. The results were paintings of subjects carefully observed, with remarkable details and imagery. By giving us such vivid representations of these Native Americans' material culture, including the extraordinarily beautiful and well-made garments they wore, Catlin affirmed that the indigenous people of this land held a highly developed aesthetic. The elaborate headdresses and quillwork and skillfully ornamented textiles and carvings depicted in his paintings are powerful evidence of how rich the cultural expressions were in Indian country.

In 1830, the year before Catlin headed west, the Indian Removal Act was passed by the United States Congress and signed into law by President Andrew Jackson. Jackson's policy was to eliminate "the Indian problem" by forcing Native Americans to give up their lands east of the Mississippi River in exchange for lands in the west. This policy sent a clear message that it was acceptable to dehumanize and marginalize Indians. While such an attitude may seem shocking to us today, at the time Indians were not allowed to vote and, in fact, were not even considered to be citizens of the United States. Our government had taken measures to ban them from speaking their languages and practicing their religions and ceremonies. The government even changed the traditional diets of the Plains Indians by encouraging the killing off of the buffalo that were so central to their way of life. During this same period, a smallpox pandemic carried by outside traders killed tens of thousands of Indians. Native Americans simply had no real power under these circumstances.

It is important for us to take this history into account when viewing George Catlin's work, and to consider his paintings within the context of the period's wars, epidemics, and removal. His work was shaped by his belief that Native peoples and their communities were being devastated by the country's rapid industrialization and westward expansion. Catlin's message that advancing civilization was destroying Indian culture is well articulated throughout his creative output, both in his art and in his writings. He hoped to show that there was a downside that came with such intense development, along with changes in the character and lives of the people who had been there for ages. Catlin's ambitions, though certainly commercial in nature, were driven by an urgency and passion to capture on canvas what Indian people looked like and where and how they lived before this was all lost for-ever. During the forty-year period spanning the years 1820–1860, over 240 treaties were made between sovereign Indian nations and the United States government, most of which required Indians to forfeit or sell off their land for significantly less than its value, thus giving up their ancestral homelands. These treaties between the tribes and the federal government provide key written source materials that inform us about this time in American history. Catlin's paintings, however, provide a visual record that informs us about even deeper complexities of the period.

Though images of Native peoples are part of this remarkable and vivid visual record, Catlin's body of work unfortunately does not provide a direct Native perspective. Catlin offered an informed outsider's viewpoint, and he clearly worked hard to express it with a high degree of integrity. However, it was far from perfect. Indeed, some contemporary historians see Catlin as someone who exploited other people's cultures. In 1832, Catlin took an especially long trip—some 2,200 miles—up the Missouri River, and in a let-ter the following year reflected on "the proud and heroic elegance of savage society, in a state of pure and original nature, beyond the reach of civilized contamination." His statement echoes the strongly held view of this period that Indians were "savages," and perhaps he had a highly romanticized idea about how Indians lived. Yet he coupled all this with empathy and human-ity. Native Americans living in the twenty-first century certainly understand this, as well as the importance of looking at their histories from multiple perspectives, including their own cultural contributions and oral traditions. The work of Catlin and other artists of the nineteenth century give all of us—whether we are Native or from another background—valuable insights into this era.

George Catlin's highly representational paintings help us understand who these people were, what they valued, and how they lived. Taken as a whole, his work reveals how well he understood and related to Indian peoples. Though Catlin lived during a profoundly tragic period of cultural destruction, when Indians were treated as if they had no future economically, politically, or culturally, his work nonetheless expresses a deep respect for his subjects. Keeping these complexities in mind as we look closely at his paintings prods us to learn more about this period of our country's history, and to do our level best to understand the many historical dynamics that influenced Catlin, and indeed all Americans at that time.

In 1837, shortly after his return from his travels to the American West, Catlin opened his Indian Gallery in New York City. On display were 474 paintings, which included 300 portraits. He subsequently took these works on tours throughout Europe at different times between 1839 and 1870. During the last half of the nineteenth century, American artists began to express more complex spiritual and moral values in their paintings. A particularly popular theme was the sublime in nature, an idea that Catlin had explored extensively in his own work years earlier. His sweeping panoramic views of the Indian landscape were also very much a precursor to the glorious American landscapes painted after the Civil War. The artist-as-traveler became a key nineteenth-century idea, and Catlin was one of the first.

As twenty-first-century people, it is impossible for us to fully transport ourselves to this different time and place. But Catlin provides us with a lens through which we can view another world, and a way to understand it better. In taking a closer look at George Catlin's artistic output, we most certainly have a good starting point for developing a deeper understanding of this complicated period of American history. Reading *Painting the Wild Frontier: The Art and Adventure of George Catlin* is an especially good place to begin!

JOHN HAWORTH

John Haworth (Cherokee) is Director of the Smithsonian National Museum of the American Indian's George Gustav Heye Center. In addition to managing public programs, exhibitions, and outreach projects, he collaborates with Native communities on a broad range of special projects. Prior to his post at the museum, he served as Assistant Commissioner for Cultural Institutions at the New York City Department of Cultural Affairs, and was on the Arts Education faculty at New York University for fourteen years. He holds an M.B.A. from Columbia University, and currently serves on the board of directors of Americans for the Arts.

PAINTING THE WILD FRONTIER

In 1778, during the Revolutionary War, a battle took place in the Wyoming Valley near Wilkes-Barre. Pennsylvania settlers and their Delaware Indian allies fought against Tory forces loyal to King George III, who were allied with the Iroquois. Many people were killed in the battle, which became known as the Wyoming Massacre.

THE WYOMING MASSACRE. PHOTOMECHANICAL PRINT: HALFTONE REPRODUCTION AFTER AN ORIGINAL PAINTING BY F.O.C. DARLEY, CA. 1905. LIBRARY OF CONGRESS.

PART ONE

First Steps on the Path, 1796–1830

>∽∾<

INDIAN TALES

Long ago, when wolves still howled in the wilderness of Pennsylvania and New York and trappers in buckskin stalked deer in the deep woods, ten-year-old George Catlin huddled close to the crackling fire and listened to his father and the other farmers trade tales of the Revolutionary War. The Wyoming Massacre was a fresh memory along the Susquehanna River in those days, and sometimes George imagined distant battle cries still echoing in the forest where he played.

The logs in the fireplace hissed and spat as Mother rocked the new baby in the cradle. George and his many brothers and sisters listened with wide eyes as Mother repeated the story of how she had been captured by Indians at the age of seven. George wondered what it would be like to meet an Indian.

He ran his fingers over the stone arrowhead he had dug up in Father's freshly plowed field, turning it over and over in his hands, feeling its flaked surface and sharp point. An Indian had made that arrowhead. If he were to meet an Indian, George wondered, would he be an enemy or a friend?

ON-O-GONG-WAY

George slipped into the forest, his older brother's rifle gripped tightly in his hands. Father would be angry that he had taken the gun without permission, but if George brought home deer meat for supper, all would be forgiven. At the salt lick near the old mill, he propped the long, heavy barrel of the rifle on a rock and waited. Soon a huge buck appeared. George gritted his teeth and took aim.

Boom!

He heard the crack and saw the flash of a gun. But it wasn't his.

The deer bounded up a hill, then tumbled to the ground and lay still. Through the clearing strode an Indian. With a large knife he slit the deer's throat and hung the animal from a tree. Then he sat on a fallen tree trunk and lit a pipe.

George crouched behind some bushes, trembling. *If he sees me, I'm lost,* he thought. *He will scalp me and devour me, and my dear mother will never know what became of me.*

For a moment he considered shooting the Indian, but then the Indian turned and George saw his face. He was just a man—no different from Father or the hired hand who worked in the wheat field.

Quietly, George backed away, then ran for home. Gasping for breath, he told his family about the Indian. At first, Mother was the only one who believed him.

The next day, George and his father found the Indian camped in the woods with his wife and daughter. Father stepped right up to them and held out his hand. Solemnly the Indian shook it. Then they smoked a pipe together. Seeing this gesture of friendship, George felt his fear melt away.

When George's mother, Polly Sutton Catlin (1770–1844), was seven years old, she and her mother were captured during the Wyoming Massacre. Luckily, they were later released unharmed.

MRS. PUTNAM CATLIN (MARY "POLLY" SUTTON), BY GEORGE CATLIN. WATERCOLOR ON IVORY, 1825. SMITHSONIAN AMERICAN ART MUSEUM. CATHERINE WALDEN MYER FUND.

In halting English, the Indian said that he was an Oneida and that his name was On-o-gong-way. His family had been driven north after the Wyoming Massacre and had resettled near the Finger Lakes of western New York, where many Oneidas and other members of the Six Nation Iroquois Confederacy lived. Now he had come back to revisit his childhood home.

"These green fields," said On-o-gong-way, ". . . were once covered with large and beautiful trees, and they were then the hunting grounds of my fathers, and they were many and strong; but we are now but a very few."

Taking George's hands in his, On-o-gong-way told George that he was a good hunter. Then he gave George some deer meat. "Your half," he said.

An awestruck George took the venison. Father told On-o-gong-way that he and his family could camp on their land as long as he wanted. George decided then and there that he wanted to get to know this Indian better.

That summer, George followed On-o-gong-way everywhere. On-o-gong-way made him a hickory bow decorated with woodpecker feathers and a new hickory handle for a tomahawk blade George had found. He showed George how to throw the tomahawk, and the boy spent hours flinging it until it stuck into the bark of a tree.

In the fall On-o-gong-way and his family decided to leave. Winter was coming, and it was time for them to return home. On-o-gong-way thanked George's family with a gift of venison and an eagle feather, and was gone.

George's father was worried. There were white men in the valley who were afraid of Indians and would shoot them on sight. Sure enough, a few days later On-o-gong-way was found dead a few miles away. He had been shot, probably by white farmers, and his wife and daughter had disappeared.

The Oneidas were one of six tribal nations that called themselves the Haudenosaunee and occupied what is now the northeastern U.S. and nearby Canadian provinces. Long before the arrival of Europeans, the Haudenosaunee had formed a powerful alliance that was later called the Iroquois Confederacy. This picture shows a nineteenth-century Iroquois tomahawk with a wooden handle and metal blade.

O-SQUÉ-SONT, OR TOMAHAWK. ENGRAVING, 1851. FROM MORGAN, LEWIS H., *LEAGUE OF THE HO-DÉ-NO-SAU-NEE, OR IROQUOIS.* ROCHESTER: SAGE & BROTHER, 1851.

No one bothered to find out who shot On-o-gong-way, and no one was ever charged with the crime. The Catlins' neighbors didn't value the life of an Indian. George was angry and upset. But there was nothing he could do.

Not long after, he was practicing with his tomahawk when it bounced off a tree and struck him on his left cheek. The wound left a deep scar, which George carried on his face for the rest of his life. His grief for On-o-gong-way left its mark, too.

SCHOOL DAYS

George Catlin was born on July 26, 1796, the fifth of Putnam and Polly Catlin's fourteen children. At the time, his family was living near Wilkes-Barre, Pennsylvania, and his father was practicing law. When George was a toddler, Putnam became a farmer. The family moved about eighty miles north, to a farm in what is now Broome County, New York, and later to Hop Bottom, Pennsylvania.

As a young child, George had lessons and chores. He also had plenty of time to play with his brothers and sisters on the farm and in the forest. When he was about eleven, his carefree days came to an end. Though he would have preferred to continue practicing his skill with the tomahawk, Father sent him and his older brothers, Charles and Henry, to boarding school in Wilkes-Barre. Classes were held in the old log courthouse. Their younger brothers, James, Julius, and Lynde, were not yet old enough to go. Their sisters, Clara, Elizabeth (Eliza), and Mary, stayed home to learn what was then considered women's work. Another sister, Juliet, had died at age two. In the years that followed, the Catlin family would continue to grow with the births of Sarah (Sally), Richard, John, and Francis.

Putnam Catlin was a descendant of Puritans, and in his strict household the father's word was final. He would eventually have nine sons, and he wanted all of them to be well educated. As for George's four sisters, reading, writing, and arithmetic would be enough. If each of the girls could learn to manage a household, raise children, live a good Christian life, and obey her husband as Polly obeyed him, Putnam would be content.

In Wilkes-Barre, George and his brothers studied English, Latin, classical Greek, geography, history, philosophy, mathematics, and "natural philosophy," or science. George's favorite subject was geography.

School life in Wilkes-Barre was not nearly as much fun as fishing, hunting, and searching for Indian arrowheads in the woods, but George did as he was told and studied hard. A gentleman had a choice of three careers in those days: doctor, lawyer, or minister. For George, Father chose law.

For a few years after graduating from the academy in Wilkes-Barre, George taught at the one-room schoolhouse in Hop Bottom while he and his family saved up enough money to pay for law school. In 1817, when he was twenty-one, George was admitted to Judge Tapping Reeve's law school in Litchfield, Connecticut, the same school his father had attended.

Litchfield was a prosperous, bustling town, and the law school was legendary. Young men flocked from all over the new nation to study with Judge Reeve, and many went on to important positions in government and industry. Women were not admitted. Instead, they attended Miss Sarah Pierce's Female Academy, where they were taught academic subjects as well as the fine arts of conversation, needlepoint, art, and music.

The law students and the young ladies took room and board in local homes, where they freely mingled. On Sundays everyone went to church together and listened to sermons by Reverend Lyman Beecher. Among the many people sitting in the pews was Reverend Beecher's little girl Harriet, who would later write *Uncle Tom's Cabin,* a famous antislavery novel.

George's father, Putnam Catlin (1764–1842), was born in Litchfield, Connecticut. He enlisted in the Continental Army at age thirteen and served for eight years. After the Revolution, Putnam studied law, then moved to Wilkes-Barre, Pennsylvania. Although he eventually turned to farming to support his growing family, he never abandoned law entirely.
Putnam Catlin, by George Catlin. Oil, 1840s. Courtesy Marjorie Catlin Stevenson, Eugene, Oregon.

This photograph shows the interior of Tapping Reeve's law school as it probably appeared when George was a student.

At law school, sitting on a hard wooden bench, George copied Judge Reeve's long lectures into notebooks, word for word. His headmaster in Wilkes-Barre had prepared him well. The other students at the law school had graduated from colleges like Yale and Princeton. George was able to keep up, even though he had not attended college. In fourteen months he filled three thousand pages with ornate script.

Though far from home, George was never far from Father's advice. Beware "the habit of writing in an ill posture," Father wrote.

Law school polished George's manners, too, for he had to be on his best behavior in the company of the young ladies from the Academy. George's older brother Charles warned him to "study closely" and not to become distracted by "girls & wine."

George's cousins Flora and Mary taught art at the Academy. From them he learned another skill in his spare time: drawing. When he wasn't poring over his law books, he liked to sketch his friends and teachers. Everyone praised his portrait of Judge Reeve.

After fourteen months of law school, George passed his exams and returned to Pennsylvania to practice. But he was beginning to realize that he was not destined to be a lawyer. "Another and stronger passion was getting the advantage of me," he wrote.

More and more, George wanted to be an artist. He knew what Father would say: Art was no profession for a gentleman.

HATCHING A PLAN

During long hours in the Pennsylvania courtroom, the young lawyer amused himself by sketching the judges, jurors, and criminals. After two years he couldn't stand the job anymore. He sold his law books and everything else he owned—except his rifle and fishing tackle—and moved to Philadelphia. There he opened a portrait-painting studio on Walnut Street.

GEORGE CATLIN, *ARTIST*, the sign proclaimed.

Father was not amused. But George was determined, and luckily he was talented, too. Ladies and gentlemen flocked to his studio, eager to commission miniature portraits of themselves, which George painted in watercolor on ivory. Before long he was considered one of the best miniature-portrait painters in town. Even Father was proud.

But George was still restless. A man who had grown up in the woods could not be content painting miniature portraits of ladies and gentlemen for the rest of his life. He missed hunting and fishing. He missed traipsing through the forest. He wanted adventure!

"My mind was continually reaching for some branch or enterprise of the art on which to devote a whole life-time of enthusiasm," he recalled.

And while George was good at painting miniatures, he knew that if he ever wanted a major career as an artist, he would have to compete with the many painters who had trained under the masters of the period: Benjamin West, John Singleton Copley, and Charles Willson Peale. West, Copley, and Peale did not paint miniatures. Their work was grand in scope and steeped in the classic traditions of European painting. West and Copley now lived in London, but Peale was right there in Philadelphia, along with his sons, the painters Raphaelle Peale, Rembrandt Peale, Rubens Peale, and Titian Peale. Another renowned portrait painter, Thomas Sully, also lived there. With that kind of competition, George would have to find a unique way to make his mark in the art world.

George often visited Charles Willson Peale's museum, on the second floor of Independence Hall. Peale's portraits of famous patriots hung on the walls, along with sketches of Indian life drawn by his son Titian. The natural-history displays featured a stuffed buffalo, a mastodon skeleton, Indian clothing and artifacts collected on Lewis and Clark's expedition, thousands of rocks and minerals, all kinds of

For many years this painting of George Catlin was thought to be a self-portrait. Now art historians think it was painted by John Neagle, a friend and roommate during the time George lived in Philadelphia. George's windblown hair and handsome features make him look like a romantic hero, full of youthful energy and optimism. He was of medium height (about five feet eight inches), thin, and muscular.
PORTRAIT OF GEORGE CATLIN, BY JOHN NEAGLE. OIL, 1825. GILCREASE MUSEUM, TULSA, OKLAHOMA.

When George moved to Philadelphia, it was the largest city in the United States, and Charles Willson Peale (1741–1827) was the most famous of the many renowned painters who lived there. Benjamin Franklin, Thomas Jefferson, and George Washington had all posed for him. Peale was also a scientist and inventor. THE ARTIST IN HIS MUSEUM, BY CHARLES WILLSON PEALE. OIL, 1822. COURTESY OF THE PENNSYLVANIA ACADEMY OF THE FINE ARTS, PHILADELPHIA. GIFT OF SARAH HARRISON (THE JOSEPH HARRISON, JR., COLLECTION).

machines, and insects, shells, coins, and stuffed curiosities from around the world, including a jackal, a mongoose, two cougars, a porcupine, an anteater, and a giraffe.

Peale, his sons, and guest scientists gave lectures in the gallery. These men believed that both art and science revealed the beauty of nature and God's divine plan. Peale's museum would become a model for George's work.

Many years later, George recalled that one day a delegation of Plains Indians arrived in Philadelphia on their way to Washington, D.C. The Indians, he wrote, were "noble and dignified-looking . . . arrayed and equipped in all their classic beauty—with shield and helmet—with tunic and manteau—tinted and tasseled off, exactly for the painter's palette! In silent and stoic dignity, these lords strutted about the city."

After the Indians left, George couldn't stop thinking about them. Would people pay to look at paintings of Indians, he wondered, the way they paid to look at the Greek statues and the paintings of Revolutionary War heroes in Peale's museum?

Maybe he could combine his talent for art with his love of adventure by painting Indians out west. It was at this moment, George later wrote, that he began to hatch a plan. It would be several years before it was fully formed.

In 1825 George moved to New York City and started to paint large portraits instead of miniatures. His work impressed Colonel William Leete Stone, a newspaper owner. Colonel Stone published some of George's drawings, introduced him to wealthy people, and hired him to make sketches of the brand-new Erie Canal for a souvenir book.

By 1826 George was able to charge forty or fifty dollars for a portrait, an amount equal to between seven hundred and nine hundred dollars today. For his huge portrait of DeWitt Clinton, the governor of New York, he was paid six hundred dollars, worth ten or eleven thousand dollars today. George's savings grew. He would need money if his plan was going to work.

During this time, George got permission from Thomas McKenney, the commissioner of Indian Affairs in Washington, D.C., to visit Indian reservations in upstate New York. There he may have sketched Seneca, Oneida, Tuscarora, Ottawa, and Mohawk Indians. These Indians had been in contact with white Europeans and Americans for centuries and no longer lived in traditional ways. George dreamed of traveling west,

A New York City street scene, a few years before George moved there. DETAIL FROM *BROADWAY AND CITY HALL*, BY AXEL KLINCKOWSTROM. LITHOGRAPH, 1819. FROM KLINCKOWSTROM, *BREF OM DE FORENTA STATERNA.* . . . STOCKHOLM: ECKSTEIN, 1824.

beyond the Mississippi River, where he could paint Indians whose lives were still relatively untouched by white civilization.

This dream was influenced by European writers and philosophers who believed that "wild" Indians were "noble savages" who had not yet been corrupted by civilization. These writers thought that life in "primitive" societies was closer to God and nature. George knew that the Indians on the New York reservations did not represent this noble ideal. But painting them was a way for him to begin to follow his dream.

Eventually, George traveled to Buffalo, New York, and painted a portrait of the famous Seneca chief Sa-go-ye-wat-ha, also known as Red Jacket. When George exhibited the painting, the white people who saw it thought Sa-go-ye-wat-ha looked ugly. They wanted Indians in paintings to look like ancient Greek heroes or the doomed characters in romantic novels.

George was not discouraged. He was determined to paint Indians, and not just in upstate New York. He wanted to paint every tribe in North America—their faces and figures, clothing, homes, weapons, ceremonies—their entire way of life. He would go west, to the Great

Plains and beyond, and paint the tribes that lived there as they always had, before Europeans had come to North America.

George didn't realize that even the Plains tribes had already been affected by contact with whites. French, English, and American fur traders had lived and traveled among the Plains Indians for years, taking out animal pelts and bringing in alcohol and disease. The introduction of guns and horses had changed the way the Indians hunted buffalo and carried out warfare between tribes. Nevertheless, it was true that Indian life beyond the Mississippi was much more traditional than that of tribes in the East.

George hoped that his paintings would rouse sympathy for the Indians. He had never forgotten his childhood friend On-o-gong-way and the fear and hatred that had caused his death.

Sometimes it seemed to George that no one cared what happened to the Indians. Most European Americans believed that white civilization was superior and that the seemingly endless resources of the vast American continent were there for them to exploit. On the East Coast, Indian tribes had been uprooted from their land, and their cultures all but destroyed. Every day, white settlers were pushing the frontier far-

While in upstate New York, George painted several landscapes of Niagara Falls, which was already a popular tourist attraction. This one is about sixteen inches high and seven feet wide.
NIAGARA FALLS, BY GEORGE CATLIN. OIL, 1827–28. SMITHSONIAN AMERICAN ART MUSEUM. GIFT OF MRS. JOSEPH HARRISON, JR.

ther west, carving farms out of the wilderness and bringing disease and destruction to the tribes that lived there. And the government did nothing to stop the settlers. In fact, it encouraged them.

George knew that the advance of European-American civilization could not be stopped. Like most white people, he believed that the Indians were doomed and that it was only a matter of time before they disappeared forever. His paintings would be a historical record, a picture of Indian life before it vanished.

George felt that the destruction of Indian cultures was a tragedy. At the same time, he saw a golden business opportunity. If he painted Indians, he would have little competition from other artists, and his exotic subject matter would bring attention to his work.

As his plan grew, he decided to collect Indian artifacts, too. They could help provide a fuller picture of how the Indians lived. He was also eager to study the geography and natural history of the Great Plains and to collect rocks and minerals.

He would follow the siren call of the wilderness. In the West he would find and depict man in his sublime natural state.

"The history and customs of such a people are themes worthy the life-time of one man," George declared, "and nothing short of the loss of my life shall prevent me from visiting their country, and of becoming their historian."

AN UNEXPECTED DEATH

To travel and paint in the West, George would need permission from the United States government and letters of introduction to important men on the frontier. He planned and plotted and saved, sharing his idea at first only with Julius, his favorite brother. Julius, eight years younger than George and a West Point graduate, had served in the United States Infantry at Fort Gibson, Arkansas Territory, on the western frontier.

Like his older brother, he had some artistic talent as well as an appetite for adventure. He thought George's plan was brilliant and promised to accompany him into the West when the time came. They would have to be well equipped and prepared to face hardship and maybe even hostile Indians. It would be a glorious expedition for two bold and daring brothers.

When Father found out about George's ambitious idea, he thought it foolish. Everyone knew the West was wild and dangerous.

Meanwhile, George was falling in love. In the spring of 1828 he married Clara Gregory, the beautiful daughter of a rich accountant whom he had met through mutual friends while visiting Albany, the capital of New York. The quiet, dark-eyed twenty-year-old Clara was swept off her feet by the handsome, self-confident thirty-one-year-old painter. George proudly took his new bride back to New York City.

Father breathed a sigh of relief. He thought George would settle down now that he was married and give up his crazy idea of traveling into the wilderness to paint Indians.

"You will now be more happy and composed," he wrote to George. ". . . In your room, and in your little parlour by your own fireside you will find contentment and solace."

But George was to find neither, for in September 1828 tragedy struck.

George had painted another portrait of Governor Clinton and had asked Julius to deliver it to Albany. On his way there, Julius stopped at a scenic waterfall and went for a swim. He was young and fit, but the current was stronger than it looked. The swirling water pulled him under, and he drowned. He was twenty-four years old.

When George heard the news, he was distraught. He blamed himself for sending Julius on the trip and believed that Julius's death was his fault. He had lost not only a brother but the friend who was to have shared his grand western adventure.

George painted this miniature portrait of Clara the year they were married. It is only two inches square. Clara was supportive, loyal, and very much in love with George. She made many sacrifices for him and his career.

CLARA BARTLETT GREGORY CATLIN (MRS. GEORGE), BY GEORGE CATLIN. WATERCOLOR, 1828. SMITHSONIAN AMERICAN ART MUSEUM. CATHERINE WALDEN MYER FUND.

George became depressed. He and Clara spent the late fall and winter in Washington, D.C., and returned to Albany for the summer. But neither his work, the change of scene, nor his pretty young wife could cheer him up.

In the months that followed, both George and Clara became ill with lung ailments. They decided to move south, to Richmond, Virginia, where the climate was milder.

There they began to recover their strength. George received a commission to paint the 101 delegates to Virginia's State Constitutional Convention. Clara became friends with Dolley Madison, the former first lady, whose miniature portrait George painted.

As he recovered from the shock of Julius's death, George once again began to dream of traveling out west to paint the Indians. He hoped such paintings would bring him money and respect, for business was slow and some art critics didn't like his work. He was good at painting faces and clothing, but sometimes his figures were awkward, the proportions of the bodies all wrong. He didn't seem to pay much attention to setting; details such as furniture or background could be vague. At times the critics' comments made him feel as if he were wasting his life.

George had to hurry. It would not be long before the traditional ways of the Great Plains Indians were destroyed by the onslaught of white settlers. The population of the United States was growing, and the eastern half of the continent was rapidly being carved into new states. Ohio already had close to a million residents, and farther west, Illinois was receiving 32,000 new settlers every year. The government encouraged the settlers and had little reason to protect the Indians.

In fact, President Andrew Jackson was about to sign the Indian Removal Act, which would force all tribes east of the Mississippi to sell their land in exchange for land in the West. George predicted disaster, for he knew that the land being given to the eastern Indians

In late 1828 George painted several Winnebago Indians who were visiting Washington, D.C. He still did not have much experience with standing figures, but this painting shows he could capture details of clothing and ornaments while also giving an overall impression of his subject through the skillful use of light and dark tones.

WAH-KÓN-ZE-KAW, THE SNAKE, BY GEORGE CATLIN. WINNEBAGO. OIL, 1828. SMITHSONIAN AMERICAN ART MUSEUM. GIFT OF MRS. JOSEPH HARRISON, JR.

already belonged to western tribes. But President Jackson echoed the beliefs of many Americans when he said, "What good man would prefer a country covered with forests and ranged by a few thousand savages to our extensive Republic, studded with cities, towns and prosperous farms?"

There was no time to waste. Though his family tried to talk him out of going, in the spring of 1830 George left Clara at her father's home in Albany and set out for St. Louis and the West.

Andrew Jackson (1767–1845) believed that Indians would never learn to live successfully among white people.
ANDREW JACKSON, PRESIDENT OF THE UNITED STATES, MARCH 4TH, 1829, BY F. KEARNY. ENGRAVING, N.D. LIBRARY OF CONGRESS.

PART TWO

The Frontier, 1830–37

◦⤙⤚◦

ST. LOUIS AND BEYOND

In St. Louis, George went straight to the office of General William Clark, governor of the Missouri Territory and superintendent of Indian Affairs. As part of the Lewis and Clark expedition many years earlier, General Clark had explored and mapped the vast western territories. He knew more about the western Indian tribes than any white man alive and possessed the most complete map of Indian territory. No white man ventured among the Indians without his permission.

George handed General Clark a letter of introduction from an official in Washington, D.C., and a portfolio filled with sketches and paintings of Indians from upstate New York. Clark was impressed. He invited George to set up an easel in his office and sketch the Indians who came to see him on tribal business. He also introduced George to important people in St. Louis, whose portrait commissions helped pay George's bills.

Expeditions into the West began in St. Louis, the center of the west-

In his home General Clark (1770–1838) had a small museum of Indian artifacts, including forty-five smoking pipes made of a special red stone that came from a quarry in what is now Minnesota.
GENERAL WILLIAM CLARK, BY GEORGE CATLIN. OIL, 1830. NATIONAL PORTRAIT GALLERY, SMITHSONIAN INSTITUTION.

ern fur trade and the most important settlement on the frontier. The town had been founded by the French in 1764 at the confluence of the Missouri and Mississippi rivers, and by 1830 it had a population of about 5,800. Down at the docks, burly men hauled pelts bound for London, Paris, Moscow, and Peking, yelling to one another in French, Spanish, English, and a score of Indian languages. Most of the pelts were beaver, which was used to make hats. Marten, otter, silver fox, and mink were also traded, as were other animal products, such as feathers, meat, grease, and tallow. The warehouses were piled high with crates of goods to be traded to the Indians: steel knives and iron pots, wool blankets and glass beads, sharp axes and sewing needles—along with guns and whiskey.

It was a rough-and-tumble place, but there were enough wealthy families to provide George with portrait work. In the meantime, he sketched and painted Indians at General Clark's side. With a few brief strokes of color George could capture the serious expression on a man's face, the intricate beading on a ceremonial robe, the gleaming edge of a tomahawk. The Indians were usually flattered that George wanted to paint their portraits. They liked the paintings, and they liked George, too, for he was open, honest, and friendly.

Ten-squát-a-way was the brother of the famous Shawnee leader Tecumseh. Years before George painted this portrait, Ten-squát-a-way had persuaded men from many tribes to join Tecumseh's fight against white settlement and in defense of Indian rights. After Ten-squát-a-way was defeated at the Battle of Tippecanoe and his brother killed during the War of 1812, their movement to unite the Indians lost momentum.

In his right hand Ten-squát-a-way holds his "medicine fire," a symbol of his spiritual power. In his left hand is a sacred string of beads.

TEN-SQUÁT-A-WAY, THE OPEN DOOR, KNOWN AS THE PROPHET, BROTHER OF TECUMSEH, BY GEORGE CATLIN. SHAWNEE. OIL, 1830. SMITHSONIAN AMERICAN ART MUSEUM. GIFT OF MRS. JOSEPH HARRISON, JR.

Still, George was restless. Even though he was painting Indians, he hadn't come all this way just to sit in an office. He was itching to get out into Indian country and explore. In July 1830 he got his chance.

With a sketchbook, a roll of canvas, a handful of brushes, and twelve colors of oil paint packed in animal bladders, George traveled with General Clark up the Mississippi River to Fort Crawford, in what is now Wisconsin. Múk-a-tah-mish-o-káh-kaik, or Black Hawk, a Sac Indian leader, was threatening war against the United States, and six tribes had asked for a treaty council. Hundreds of Indians were camped about the fort, and George could hear their songs and see their fires burning late into the night. He wandered happily among them, sketchbook in hand. The Indians accepted his presence, although George probably didn't paint any of their portraits. If he did, none survived.

That fall George took a boat up the Missouri River to Fort Leavenworth, near present-day Kansas City, Kansas, where he painted men from eight different tribes. Years later he wrote about taking yet another trip, during which he rode west on horseback through the tall prairie grass to visit Konsa villages in what is now the state of Kansas. There, he said, the dogs yelped at his horse, the chiefs welcomed him with a pipe, and the women fed him buffalo meat.

As he traveled, George sketched and took notes on everything he saw. He was getting a taste of life

Kee-món-saw's clothing shows that his tribe, the Kaskaskia, had been in contact with Europeans and Americans for many years. By 1830 the Kaskaskias, fleeing the advance of white civilization, had given up their land in Illinois and resettled first in what is now Missouri and Arkansas, then in Kansas.

Kee-món-saw holds a kind of wooden flute that was used by men to court women. This portrait, like the previous one, was probably painted at Fort Leavenworth.

KEE-MÓN-SAW, LITTLE CHIEF, A CHIEF, BY GEORGE CATLIN. KASKASKIA. OIL, 1830. SMITHSONIAN AMERICAN ART MUSEUM. GIFT OF MRS. JOSEPH HARRISON, JR.

among the Plains Indians, whose traditional ways he knew would not last much longer. Every year the fur traders were slaughtering buffalo and other game that the native peoples depended on for food. They were giving liquor to the Indians and introducing diseases to which the Indians had no resistance. And they were supplying the Indians with guns, which some tribes turned against one another. If George was going to paint all the tribes, he would have to paint fast.

George spent most of 1831 back in the East and returned to St. Louis in December. By spring he was ready to begin his epic voyage up the Missouri on the steamboat *Yellowstone*.

THE VOYAGE OF THE *YELLOWSTONE*

In March 1832 George watched from the deck of the *Yellowstone* as St. Louis disappeared in the distance. It was the steamboat's maiden voyage up the Missouri River. A lot was at stake for its owner, the American Fur Company. If the boat made it to Fort Union, two thousand miles upstream, it would mean huge profits, for she could go much faster and hold more cargo than the small flatboats that usually made the trip, pushed upriver with poles. The American Fur Company's goal was to dominate the fur trade throughout the West by overwhelming its main competitors, the Rocky Mountain Fur Company and the Hudson's Bay Company.

In 1832 the demand for beaver fur and buffalo skins knew no bounds. Every day the hunt was pushing trappers farther into the western frontier. Rivers served as highways back then, and the muddy Missouri was the most important river of all. For thousands of miles west and north of St. Louis, the Missouri threaded its way through the endless prairie, its brown waters flanked at times by tall clay bluffs. George thought their water-carved forms resembled the ruins of an ancient city.

The *Yellowstone* made slow progress against the swift current as she steered around sandbars, snags, and huge pieces of driftwood. George set up his easel on the deck and painted the landscape as it unfolded. When he wasn't painting, he wrote in his notebook. All around the boat, the muddy water churned.

The boat's first destination was Fort Tecumseh, twelve hundred miles northwest of St. Louis, near present-day Pierre, South Dakota. Two hundred miles before she reached the fort, the *Yellowstone* ran aground on a sandbar. The men tried to haul her off with ropes, but she wouldn't budge. For a week they waited for rain to raise the water level of the river. Finally, a group of trappers on board decided they had been stranded long enough. If they couldn't get to the fort by boat, they would go on foot, two hundred miles through Indian country. The boat could catch up with them when the rain came.

This painting shows the *Yellowstone* as she embarks from St. Louis on her first trip to the Upper Missouri. With her wood-burning engines and shallow draft, the boat was specially built to navigate the river. Although the presence of Indians on the boat is accurate, most of the whites on board were French-Canadian trappers and men hired to do manual work at the forts along the river, not the well-dressed ladies and gentlemen shown here.

ST. LOUIS FROM THE RIVER BELOW, BY GEORGE CATLIN. OIL, 1832–33. SMITHSONIAN AMERICAN ART MUSEUM. GIFT OF MRS. JOSEPH HARRISON, JR.

George slung his rifle and art supplies onto his back and set off with the trappers across the prairie. He had heard there were Western Sioux (Lakota) Indians camped at Fort Tecumseh, and nothing was going to stop him from painting them.

As they marched through Lakota Sioux country, George struggled to keep up with the trappers. He was young and strong, but the rugged frontiersmen kept a swift pace up and down the rolling green hills. It was easy for George to be distracted by the beauties of the prairie—the wind whooshing through the tall grass, the broad blue sky, the sweet scent of spring flowers—and he couldn't resist stopping occasionally to examine the rocks. If he found a particularly interesting specimen, he would slip it into his pocket. He knew it was wise to be on the lookout, though most Indians in these parts were friendly. But there were rattlers here, and a man who accidentally came between a female grizzly and her cubs could be ripped to shreds.

Try as he might, the landscape was just too alluring. George soon fell behind.

Luckily, one of the trappers took pity on him and told him to stop walking with his toes turned out like a city man. Whether he also reminded him about the dangers that surrounded them, George didn't say. From then on, George kept up with the others.

When the men were hungry, they stopped to shoot buffalo, elk, or antelope, roasting the meat on a campfire and washing it down with gulps of black coffee. On the tenth day, as they approached Fort Tecumseh, George's heart beat faster when he saw the thousands of Lakota Sioux camped around the fort. He was eager to start painting them. The trappers, however, had other ideas. They strode right past the Indians and into the fort, which was two hundred feet square and surrounded by high wooden palisades. Inside were log cabins, shops, workrooms, storage sheds, and accommodations for horses and other animals. Many of the fur company employees had Indian wives and children, who lived with them in the fort.

The next day, George found out that painting the Lakota Sioux would not be so easy. The Lakotas had never seen portraits on canvas before. They were suspicious and even afraid of George. If he was going to paint them, he would first have to win their trust.

The western fur trade was originally conducted at once-a-year outdoor gatherings, called rendezvous, at which Indians, fur company representatives, and trappers, or mountain men, got together to trade, gamble, and drink. By the late 1820s the American Fur Company had decided that fixed locations would be better for business and had built a series of fortified trading posts, like this one, along the Missouri and Platte rivers. During George's visit, Fort Tecumseh was renamed Fort Pierre.

THE LAKOTAS SIT FOR THEIR PORTRAITS

George asked to meet in private with one of the Lakota chiefs, Ha-wón-je-tah, or One Horn. Ha-wón-je-tah strode into George's painting room, handsome and confident in his elk-skin shirt, his long hair piled atop his head like a turban.

Would he let George paint his portrait?

The chief looked into George's eyes and said yes.

When the portrait was finished, George recalled, Ha-wón-je-tah called him a "medicine painter." What the chief meant was that George's painting had demonstrated a kind of magic or spiritual power. George hung the painting outside for all to see.

The Indians were shocked. Some trembled in fear, saying George had taken away Ha-wón-je-tah's face. Soon there were rumors among the medicine men that bad luck, even death, would befall any man who let himself be painted. The medicine men, who were greatly respected for their spiritual powers, predicted that Ha-wón-je-tah would not be able to sleep at night, because in the picture his eyes were always open. George had to work hard to convince Ha-wón-je-tah that he was not in danger. Fortunately, the chief believed George, and no harm befell him. Afterward, some of the men were willing to sit for their portraits.

George fell to work at a furious pace, painting as many as six portraits a day. Over a broad wash of background color he outlined his figures in quick strokes, then filled in the faces and upper bodies. With touches of blue and red he showed details of costume and headdress, leaving the paint thin, so it could dry quickly. He would finish the paintings later, adding more detail back east in his studio.

Though George would have liked to paint the Indian women who were camped at the fort, he later wrote that the Lakota men scoffed at the idea. George had told them that the portraits were for "white chiefs, to show who were the most distinguished and worthy of the

Ha-wón-je-tah's name, One Horn (or One Shell), came from the small shell that hung around his neck, which he treasured because it had belonged to his father. His clothing was made of elk skins, fringed with porcupine quills and scalp locks. Like their white counterparts, almost all the Indians who posed for George wore their finest clothing.

HA-WÓN-JE-TAH, ONE HORN, HEAD CHIEF OF THE MINICONJOU TRIBE, BY GEORGE CATLIN. WESTERN SIOUX/LAKOTA. OIL, 1832. SMITHSONIAN AMERICAN ART MUSEUM. GIFT OF MRS. JOSEPH HARRISON, JR.

The Lakota Sioux ate dog meat only on special ceremonial occasions. The animals were kept primarily as watchdogs and for hunting. They also helped to pull belongings from camp to camp.

Sioux Dog Feast, by George Catlin. Oil, 1832–37. Smithsonian American Art Museum. Gift of Mrs. Joseph Harrison, Jr.

Sioux." If these were portraits of men, for men, why would he want to paint women?

George *did* want to paint women, but as a white man of his time, he was used to thinking of women as less important than men. He told the Lakota men that he wanted to show the white chiefs how the Lakota women looked and dressed. He said that the women's portraits would hang *under* those of their husbands. But not many of the men were convinced, and George was able to paint only a few women.

Did the Indian women remind him of the woman he had left behind in Albany? Did he miss his wife? He didn't say.

Some days later the *Yellowstone* finally arrived, and the fort was renamed Fort Pierre in honor of Pierre Chouteau, manager of the American Fur Company's western operations. The Lakotas joined in celebrating the naming of the fort with a feast of dog meat, which George politely declined to eat. But he did paint the feast.

He painted the Lakota dances, too, thrilled by the fierce stamping and jumping, the chants and loud cries. But on his last day at Fort Pierre, George painted a portrait that caused him to be condemned to death.

THE DOG VS. LITTLE BEAR

All day long the Indians had been sitting around the edges of George's painting room, watching silently as the "medicine painter" created portraits—each man waiting his turn in order of his importance in the tribe. This day the Indians seemed uneasy, and George noticed that one man, named Shón-ka, The Dog, sat apart.

The trouble started when George decided to paint Mah-tó-che-ga, Little Bear, so that only three quarters of his face could be seen. When the painting was done, Shón-ka lurched forward, a sneer on his lips.

"Mah-tó-che-ga is but half a man!" said Shón-ka.

"Who says that?" demanded Mah-tó-che-ga.

"Shón-ka says it. And Shón-ka can prove it." Shón-ka pointed to George. "He knows you are but *half a man,* for he has painted but half of your face and knows that the other half is good for nothing!"

"You are nothing but an old woman and a coward," roared Mah-tó-che-ga, and he stalked out of the fort to his tipi, where he loaded his rifle, for he intended to shoot Shón-ka. But first, Mah-tó-che-ga prayed. And while he prayed, his wife shook the lead ball out of his rifle, thinking to prevent a murder.

Shón-ka had a rifle, too, and when the two men found each other, they both shot at once. Ironically, half of Mah-tó-che-ga's face was blown away, and he died.

Immediately, a war cry went up in the camp as Mah-tó-che-ga's band vowed revenge. They would kill Shón-ka, and if they couldn't catch Shón-ka, they would kill George instead, for wasn't his painting the cause of Mah-tó-che-ga's death?

When the traders inside the fort heard the commotion, they slammed the gates shut and prepared for an assault. Night fell, and war chants filled the air. George rolled up his canvases, shoved his paints, brushes, and notebooks into his pack, and prepared to fight for his life. But the superintendent of the fort advised him to flee, and in the early hours of the morning George slipped out of the fort and boarded the *Yellowstone.* In silence she steamed up the river, bound for Fort Union, at the mouth of the Yellowstone River in what is now western North Dakota. George could only hope that Mah-tó-che-ga's relatives would not follow.

MEN OF LONG HAIR AND GREAT DEEDS

When Mah-tó-che-ga's relatives saw that George had escaped, they jumped onto their horses and raced after him. George was lucky. The Indians broke off their pursuit when they realized that their horses couldn't catch the boat.

LEFT: The portrait that started all the trouble. George had no idea that painting Mah-tó-che-ga in partial profile would lead to the Indian's death.
MAH-TÓ-CHE-GA, LITTLE BEAR, A HUNKPAPA BRAVE, BY GEORGE CATLIN. WESTERN SIOUX/LAKOTA. OIL, 1832. SMITHSONIAN AMERICAN ART MUSEUM. GIFT OF MRS. JOSEPH HARRISON, JR.

RIGHT: While Mah-tó-che-ga gazes into the distance with a furrowed brow, Shón-ka looks directly at the viewer. Perhaps his stern expression and haughty bearing give some insight into his personality, providing a clue as to why he chose to pick a fight with Mah-tó-che-ga.
SHÓN-KA, THE DOG, CHIEF OF THE BAD ARROW POINTS BAND, BY GEORGE CATLIN. WESTERN SIOUX/LAKOTA. OIL, 1832. SMITHSONIAN AMERICAN ART MUSEUM. GIFT OF MRS. JOSEPH HARRISON, JR.

As the *Yellowstone* continued upriver, she passed Ponca and other Indian villages where no one had seen a steamboat before. With smoke pouring from her smokestacks, the captain would blast cannons as a salute, frightening the villagers. Not understanding how the boat was powered or steered, the Indians thought that it was driven by mysterious supernatural powers. George wrote that they called it "the big thunder canoe" or the "big medicine canoe with eyes."

A few days later, George was welcomed to Fort Union by Kenneth McKenzie, the American Fur Company agent and so-called King of the Upper Missouri, with a feast of buffalo tongue, beaver tail, and aged wine. By now it was high summer, and five or six different tribes had come to the fort to trade, their painted buffalo-skin tipis dotting the prairie. In a room he set up as a studio, George sat on the long breech of a cannon and painted Blackfoot, Crow, Ojibwa, Cree, and Assiniboine Indians.

This print, based on a drawing by John Mix Stanley, shows Indians trading at Fort Union. Stanley worked throughout the West beginning in 1839, hoping to build a collection that could be shown in eastern cities. But he lacked George's theatrical flair, and by the time he exhibited his paintings, Indian scenes were not as popular as they once had been.

FORT UNION, AND DISTRIBUTION OF GOODS TO THE ASSINNIBOINES [SIC]. COLOR LITHOGRAPH, CA. 1855. SARONY, MAJOR & KNAPP, AFTER AN ORIGINAL DRAWING BY JOHN MIX STANLEY. LIBRARY OF CONGRESS.

Tcha-aés-ka-ding, grandson of the Blackfoot chief Stu-mick-o-súcks, poses with his bow and arrows and a raccoon-skin robe, wearing only a breechcloth and moccasins. By practicing archery from an early age, boys developed skills that would one day enable them to provide food and defend against enemies.

TCHA-AÉS-KA-DING, GRANDSON OF BUFFALO BULL'S BACK FAT, BY GEORGE CATLIN. BLACKFOOT/KAINAI. OIL, 1832. SMITHSONIAN AMERICAN ART MUSEUM. GIFT OF MRS. JOSEPH HARRISON, JR.

"The Crows and Blackfeet who are here together, are enemies of the most deadly kind," he wrote, ". . . but here they sit and smoke quietly together."

Still, George was glad that the Indians' weapons had been taken away when they entered the fort, for he couldn't help but notice their "sidelong looks of deep-rooted hatred."

Over the following weeks, a procession of magnificently dressed men sat patiently for their portraits. First to be painted was Stu-mick-o-súcks, Buffalo Bull's Back Fat, a Blackfoot chief. His name refers to the hump of the buffalo, which was considered the tastiest cut of meat. The stem of Stu-mick-o-súcks's red stone pipe was over four feet long and decorated with braided porcupine quills. His deerskin shirt was fringed with scalp locks—"black hair," George wrote, "which he has taken from the heads of victims slain by his own hand in battle."

Later, George painted Peh-tó-pe-kiss, Eagle's Ribs; Mix-ke-móte-skin-na, Iron Horn; Tcha-dés-sa-ko-máh-pee, Bear's Child; Cháh-ee-chópes, Four Wolves; and even one of Stu-mick-o-súcks's wives, Eeh-nís-kim, Crystal Stone, and his grandson, Tcha-aés-ka-ding. The curious crowd grew so large that the chiefs had to station men with spears at the door to protect George and give him room to work. Several chiefs from each tribe decided who was worthy of the honor of being painted.

George often visited the Indians in their tipis, where the men would boast of their courageous deeds in battle and tell stories of the hunt. He also learned about their spiritual beliefs and leaders, the medicine men.

These greatly respected individuals played important roles in religious ceremonies and used their knowledge of herbs and roots to heal the sick.

George learned, too, that religious practice was not limited to medicine men. Every man, he wrote, began to develop his spiritual powers during adolescence.

A boy, at the age of fourteen or fifteen years, is said to be "making or forming his medicine" when he wanders away from his father's lodge and absents himself for the space of two or three, and sometimes even four or five, days; lying on the ground in some remote or secluded spot, crying to the Great Spirit, and fasting the whole time.

According to George, the boy would wait for a special dream that would reveal which bird, reptile, or other animal was to be his protecting spirit throughout life.

He then returns home to his father's lodge, and relates his success; and after allaying his thirst, and satiating his appetite, he searches for the animal with weapons or traps . . . the skin of which he reserves entire, and ornaments it according to his own fancy, and carries it with him through life.

As he spent time among them, George came to particularly admire the Crow and Blackfoot men, describing them as "cleanly in their persons, elegant in their dress and manners, and enjoying life to the greatest perfection."

This Blackfoot medicine man is ministering to a chief who has been shot. George described the scene in great detail in his writings, but for some reason he chose to paint only the medicine man, not the dying chief.

The medicine man wears wears the entire skin of a yellow bear, including the head and claws. George wrote that a medicine man's outfit was often decorated with "the skins of snakes, and frogs, and bats—beaks and toes and tails of birds—hoofs of deer, goats, and antelope; and in fact, the 'odds and ends' and fag ends, and tails, and tips of almost everything that swims, flies, or runs, in this part of the wide world."

MEDICINE MAN, PERFORMING HIS MYSTERIES OVER A DYING MAN, BY GEORGE CATLIN. BLACKFOOT/SIKSIKA. OIL, 1832. SMITHSONIAN AMERICAN ART MUSEUM. GIFT OF MRS. JOSEPH HARRISON, JR.

A label from a container of chewing tobacco. Nineteenth-century manufacturers used images of buffalo hunting to associate their products with the romance of the Wild West.
RIVALS. CHEWING TOBACCO. SPENCE BROTHERS AND CO., CINCINNATI, OHIO. COLOR LITHOGRAPH, CA. 1872. STROBRIDGE & CO. LIBRARY OF CONGRESS.

"The present chief of the Crows . . . is called 'Long-hair,' and has received his name as well as his office from the circumstance of having the longest hair of any man in the nation," George wrote. ". . . Ten feet and seven inches in length."

This chief usually folded his hair into a block, which he carried under his arm or inside his robe. But on special occasions he would let it drag on the ground three or four feet behind him, "black and shining like a raven's wing."

Among the Assiniboines, George saw many games and amusements, including dancing, horseracing, and a ball game similar to lacrosse. He shared many meals in the Indian camps, too, dining on buffalo meat flavored with herbs, roots, wild greens, or berries. Whites and Indians alike prized buffalo meat more than any other kind. Before long, George learned that nothing was more exciting than the buffalo hunt.

"GOING FOR MEAT"

Almost every day, when he was not painting, George rode out to watch and sketch the Indians hunting buffalo. Sometimes the hunters would creep up to the herd on foot, but most often they attacked on horseback, shooting the buffalo with arrows or spearing them with long lances while galloping at full speed. The whites hunted on horseback, too, but with rifles. Both whites and Indians took great pride in their hunting skills.

One fine morning the superintendent of the fort announced that it was time to "go for meat." George saddled up his favorite horse and grabbed his rifle.

"We all crossed the river, and galloped away a couple of miles or so, where we mounted the bluff," he wrote. "There was a fine herd of some four or five hundred buffaloes, perfectly at rest. We advanced within a mile or so, and came to a halt."

Someone tossed a feather into the air to figure out which way the wind was blowing. Then the men took off their hats and coats, rolled up their sleeves, and loaded their pockets with bullets. A few threw extra bullets into their mouths.

Slowly, the riders approached the herd. One buffalo lifted its head, then another. Suddenly, as if an alarm bell had gone off, the buffalo began to run.

"Away all sailed, and over the prairie flew, in a cloud of dust which was raised by their trampling hoofs," wrote George.

George galloped after a huge bull.

Boom!

George's bullet lodged in the buffalo's shoulder, and the great beast

Hiding under a wolf skin, a hunter could creep among the herd until he was close enough to shoot a buffalo in the heart. This would kill the animal quickly, before it could turn on its attacker.
BUFFALO HUNT UNDER THE WOLF-SKIN MASK, BY GEORGE CATLIN. OIL, 1832–33. SMITHSONIAN AMERICAN ART MUSEUM. GIFT OF MRS. JOSEPH HARRISON, JR.

sank to its knees. Seeing it was injured and could not attack him with its horns, George rode up to take a closer look.

"At my approach he wheeled around—and bristled up for battle," George wrote. "He seemed to know perfectly well that he could not escape from me, and resolved to meet his enemy and death as bravely as possible."

The animal was suffering, and George knew it. He could have killed it right away with another bullet. Instead, he laid his gun across his lap, pulled his sketchbook out of his pocket, and began to draw the dying bull. He had sworn to draw every aspect of life on the Great Plains— and that meant drawing death as well.

I rode around him and sketched him . . . sometimes he would lie down, and I would then sketch him; then throw my cap at

In the interest of his art, George allowed this buffalo to suffer so that he could sketch it while it was dying. Most Indians would have considered his actions shamefully disrespectful. The finished painting shows the animal shot with an arrow instead of with a bullet.

DYING BUFFALO, SHOT WITH AN ARROW, BY GEORGE CATLIN. OIL, 1832–33. SMITHSONIAN AMERICAN ART MUSEUM. GIFT OF MRS. JOSEPH HARRISON, JR.

him, and rousing him on his legs, rally a new expression, and
sketch him again.

In this way I added to my sketchbook some invaluable
sketches of this grim-visaged monster. . . .

I defy the world to produce another animal that can look so
frightful as a huge buffalo bull, when wounded as he was,
turned around for battle, and swelling with rage; —his eyes
bloodshot, and his long shaggy mane hanging to the ground,
—his mouth open, and his horrid rage hissing in streams of
smoke and blood from his mouth and through his nostrils,
as he is bending forward to spring upon his assallant.

After a while, the other hunters approached on foot, leading their
exhausted horses. Dead buffalo lay about them on the plain, to be
picked up later and hauled back to the fort in carts. George put away
his sketchbook and ended his buffalo's life with a shot to the head.

DOWN THE MISSOURI

Soon the *Yellowstone* steamed back to St. Louis. George stayed on at
Fort Union, thinking he would canoe back to St. Louis by himself, two
thousand miles downstream. When the superintendent reminded him
that there were hostile tribes along the way, George changed his plan,
but only a little. In mid-July he bought a small skiff and a couple of
paddles and set off for St. Louis with two French trappers, Jean Ba'tiste
and Abraham Bogard. With them went George's painting gear and
Indian clothing; rifles and ammunition; food, including a some dried
buffalo tongues and two dozen beaver tails; and three tin cups, a cof-
feepot, one plate, a frying pan, and a tin kettle. By now George had
learned to dress in buckskin, because it shed water better than woven
cloth and lasted much longer.

British artist William Fisk painted this portrait of George as he imagined him to have looked in 1832. In reality, George would have looked much younger. The figures in the background are based on George's portraits of the Blackfoot Indians Mix-ke-móte-skin-na, Iron Horn, and Ah'-kay-ee-pix-en, Woman Who Strikes Many, both of whom he painted at Fort Union.

GEORGE CATLIN, BY WILLIAM FISK. OIL, 1849. NATIONAL PORTRAIT GALLERY, SMITHSONIAN INSTITUTION. GIFT OF MAY C. KINNEY, ERNEST C. KINNEY, AND BRADFORD WICKES.

The first night they camped among thousands of Assiniboines. After that they saw no one for several days. When they weren't paddling, they drifted with the current, and when they grew tired of drifting, they stopped to hunt and fish. At night they beached the skiff, unrolled their blankets, and slept on the ground under the vast night sky.

Sometimes George would land the boat and climb a hill to admire and paint the scenery. He especially liked the view "at *sun-set;* when the green hill-tops are turned into gold—and their long shadows of melancholy are thrown over the valleys—when all the breathings of day are hushed, and nought but the soft notes of the dove can be heard."

During his trip down the Missouri in 1832, George painted many landscapes. The high river bluffs provided shapes and colors that delighted the painter's eye. In contrast, the flat prairie seemed to him like an endless green sea, monotonous and difficult to capture on canvas.

THE THREE DOMES, CLAY BLUFFS 15 MILES ABOVE THE MANDAN VILLAGE, BY GEORGE CATLIN. OIL, 1832. SMITHSONIAN AMERICAN ART MUSEUM. GIFT OF MRS. JOSEPH HARRISON, JR.

This photograph shows the exterior of a traditional Mandan home.
MANDAN EARTHEN LODGE, BY EDWARD S. CURTIS. PHOTOGRAPH, CA. 1908. LIBRARY OF CONGRESS.

One morning George, Ba'tiste, and Bogard awoke to find a female grizzly bear and her two cubs staring at them. They could see from the bear's footprints that she had sniffed them while they slept. Worse, she had pawed through the skiff and eaten all their food. Carefully, they climbed into the skiff and pushed off from the bank while the grizzlies watched. George didn't worry about the lost food. He knew the prairie would supply them with plenty to eat.

When George and his companions finally arrived at the fur company outpost of Fort Clark (about sixty miles north of present-day Bismarck, North Dakota), they were glad to see friendly people. Nearby was a Mandan village, and George was hoping the Mandans would let him paint their portraits. He had heard some intriguing stories about their sacred ceremonies and traditions, and he wanted to learn more about their cultures.

AMONG THE MANDANS

Like the other Plains tribes, the Mandans had never seen portrait paintings. To put them at ease, George first painted two chiefs, setting up his

This print, based on a drawing by Swiss artist Karl Bodmer, shows the inside of a Mandan home. Bodmer painted portraits of some of the same people as George, including Stu-mick-o-súcks and Máh-to-tóh-pa.

THE INTERIOR OF THE HUT OF A MANDAN CHIEF. ENGRAVING AFTER AN ORIGINAL DRAWING BY KARL BODMER, N.D. LIBRARY OF CONGRESS.

easel inside one of the Mandans' dirt-and-timber houses. When the chiefs saw the paintings, they stared at them for a long time. *"Te-ho-pe-nee Wash-ee!"* they whispered. "Medicine White Man."

According to George, the chiefs shook George's hand and went back to their lodges, where they smoked a sacred stone pipe and gradually began to tell others about the paintings.

"A throng of women and girls were about my house," George wrote, "and through every crack and crevice I could see their glistening eyes." Before long, the women surrounded the house "like a swarm of bees hanging on the front and sides of their hive."

At first the men hung back. Then curiosity overcame them. So many people wanted to see the paintings that George asked one of the fur traders to hold up the canvases outside the door. As soon as he did so, the Indians began to yell.

"Some were stamping off in the jarring dance—," George wrote, "others were singing, and others again were crying—hundreds covered their mouths with their hands and were mute; others, indignant, drove their spears frightfully into the ground, and some shot a reddened arrow at the sun, and went home to their wigwams."

The crowd demanded to see George. He didn't know if it was safe, but out he came. Men shook his hand, saying he was "the greatest *medicine-man* in the world." Children crept between the legs of the adults and reached out to touch him.

But the women were frightened and hung back. They thought his paintings were alive, and "commenced a mournful and doleful chaunt [*sic*] against me," George wrote, "crying and weeping bitterly through the village, proclaiming me a most dangerous man." The women said he should leave the village immediately, before he brought bad luck.

A tribal council was held. George told the men that he was a human being like themselves and that anyone who practiced could learn to paint the way he did. He reminded them that he came in friendship, and said that in the white man's country, "brave men never allowed their [women] to frighten them with their foolish whims and stories."

That did it, according to George; most of the men were ready to be painted. The rest sat around smoking their pipes, keeping an eye on him.

George painted the men according to rank, complimenting each on his good looks. Afterward, he was invited to a feast and given a doctor's rattle and a staff strung with grizzly-bear claws, antelope hooves, ermine, wild sage, and bat wings, "perfumed with the choice and savoury odor" of skunk. This was considered a great honor.

Still, some men would not sit for their portraits. They were convinced that doing so would bring certain death.

George stayed with the Mandans for weeks—painting, writing, and observing. He became friends with Máh-to-tóh-pa, Four Bears, second chief of the tribe, who gave George a shirt on which the chief had painted scenes of the great battles of his life. George praised Máh-to-tóh-pa's "grace and manly dignity" and wrote that he posed for hours "with the stillness of a statue."

As George painted, life went on around him. The Mandan women worked continually, he observed, "procuring wood and water . . .

Twelve-year-old Sha-kó-ka shows off her gray hair. About ten percent of Mandans had gray hair, even in childhood. It was a hereditary characteristic.

SHA-KÓ-KA, MINT, A PRETTY GIRL, BY GEORGE CATLIN. MANDAN/NUMAKIKI. OIL, 1832. SMITHSONIAN AMERICAN ART MUSEUM. GIFT OF MRS. JOSEPH HARRISON, JR.

dressing robes and other skins . . . drying meat and wild fruit, and . . . raising corn (maize)." Each man had many wives, and "the one who [had] the greatest number of wives [was] considered the most affluent and envied man in the tribe."

During this time, George also visited and painted the Hidatsa Indians, whose villages lay eight miles upriver from the Mandans. George happened to have an old newspaper with him, and when the Hidatsas saw him reading it, they thought that staring at a newspaper must be some kind of medical treatment. They called the newspaper "the medicine cloth for sore eyes."

While in the Hidatsa village, George joined a horserace and also painted some visiting Crow chiefs. George thought the Crows wore the most beautiful clothes of any he had seen.

"No part of the human race," he wrote, "could present a more picturesque and thrilling appearance on horseback than a party of Crows, rigged out in all their plumes and trappings."

In his letters, which were published back east in Colonel Stone's two New York newspapers, George described the Mandan horseraces and archery competitions, their steam baths and bathing rituals. He wrote about the buffalo dance, the scalp dance, and the rain dance, and he described how the Mandans visited with their dead relatives, whose skulls were placed in sacred circles on the prairie.

These people never bury the dead, but place the bodies on slight scaffolds just above the reach of human hands, and out of the way of wolves and dogs; and they are there left to moulder and decay. . . .

Some hundreds of these bodies may be seen reposing in this manner in this curious place, which the Indians call, "the village of the dead." . . .

When the scaffolds on which the bodies rest, decay and fall to the ground, the nearest relations having buried the rest of the bones, take the skulls, which are perfectly bleached and purified, and place them in circles of an hundred or more on the prairie. . . .

In the center of each ring or circle is a little mound of three feet high, on which uniformly rest two buffalo skulls (a male and female); and in the center of the little mound is erected a "medicine pole." . . . Here then, to this strange place do these people again resort . . . fond affections and endearments are here renewed, and conversations are here held and cherished with the dead.

The Mandan ceremony that most impressed George was the *O-kee-pa*, in which the young men of the tribe endured painful, bloody rituals in order to please the Great Spirit, ward off the Evil Spirit, ensure good hunting, and prove their readiness to defend the tribe. About fifty young men participated.

"Each one's body was chiefly naked," George wrote, "and covered with clay of different colours; some were red, others were yellow, and some were covered with white clay. . . . Each one of them carried in his

George wrote that the Mandans showed as much care, respect, and affection for their dead relatives and friends as white people did. When he saw that people of different races and civilizations shared such feelings, he felt he had been given a moral lesson.
BACK VIEW OF MANDAN VILLAGE, SHOWING THE CEMETERY, BY GEORGE CATLIN. OIL, 1832. SMITHSONIAN AMERICAN ART MUSEUM. GIFT OF MRS. JOSEPH HARRISON, JR.

right hand his medicine-bag—on his left arm, his shield of bull's hide—in his left hand, his bow and arrows, with his quiver slung on his back."

George was ushered into the medicine lodge, where the most secret parts of the ritual would take place. In the dim light he could see human and buffalo skulls arranged on the floor, along with four tortoise-shaped drums that were said to contain water from the four quarters of the earth. A sacred object resembling a tortoise sat on a scaffold in the center of the room. A medicine man was in charge.

> *It was his duty to lie by a small fire in the centre of the lodge, with his medicine-pipe in his hand, crying to the Great Spirit incessantly, watching the young men, and preventing entirely their escape from the lodge, and all communication whatever with people outside, for the space of four days and nights, during which time they were not allowed to eat, to drink, or to sleep, preparatory to the excruciating self-tortures which they were to endure on the fourth day. . . .*
>
> *On the floor of the lodge was placed a knife, and by the side of it a bundle of splints or skewers, which were kept in readiness for the infliction of the cruelties directly to be explained. There were seen also, in this stage of the affair, a number of cords of rawhide hanging down from the top of the lodge, and passing through its roof, with which the young men were to be suspended by the splints passed through their flesh, and drawn up by men placed on the top of the lodge for the purpose.*

George was the first white man to create pictures of the *O-kee-pa* from inside the spirit lodge, and his sketches, paintings, and written descriptions of the ceremonies are famous. They are the most detailed record of the *O-kee-pa* in existence, and without them we would know little about it.

In 1837, five years after George's visit, almost the entire Mandan tribe was wiped out by smallpox.

After almost four days of fasting in the medicine lodge, *O-kee-pa* participants had splints driven through their flesh. They were then suspended in the air until they fainted. The ritual was a test of manhood.

The Cutting Scene, Mandan O-kee-pa Ceremony, by George Catlin. Oil, 1832. Denver Art Museum: The William Sr. and Dorothy Harmsen Collection, 2001.456 © Denver Art Museum.

BLACK HAWK IN CHAINS

As summer ended, George shipped paintings, Indian articles, minerals, and fossils back to St. Louis. Then he, Ba'tiste, and Bogard continued their voyage down the Missouri, stopping to paint several other tribes along the way.

As autumn came, the grasses of the prairie ripened into gold. George marveled at the numbers of birds, insects, and other animals, and especially at the size of the buffalo herds. Once, the skiff came upon a herd as it was crossing the river.

"We had heard the 'roaring' . . . of the herd when we were several miles from them," he wrote. "When we came in sight, we were actually terrified at the immense numbers that were streaming down the green hills on one side of the river, and galloping up and over the bluffs on the other. The river was filled, and in parts blackened, with their heads and horns, as they were swimming about."

The men had to beach the skiff and wait for the herd to pass. There were so many buffalo that it took several hours.

On another day they came upon a war party of Arikara Indians, and he and his companions had to make a quick getaway in the skiff. They were so scared that they paddled all day and all night. When they finally stopped, they were attacked by mosquitoes. They scrambled up a hill and took shelter under a buffalo robe. It began to rain, then pour. In the morning they found themselves at the edge of a cliff and had to sit in the slippery mud until the sun dried it, or else they would have fallen into the river a hundred feet below.

They finally reached Fort Pierre, where George sketched Cheyenne and Nez Perce Indians and avoided the relatives of Shón-ka and Mah-tó-che-ga, who were still after him. Later he climbed "Floyd's Grave," a bluff where Sergeant Floyd, a member of the Lewis and Clark expedition, was buried.

From its top [I could see] the windings infinite of the Missouri, its thousand hills and domes of green, vanishing into blue in distance, when nought but the soft-breathing winds were heard, to break the stillness and quietude of the scene. Where not the chirping of bird or sound of cricket, nor soaring eagle's scream, were interposed 'tween God and man.

As he gazed at the beautiful landscape, George imagined what the wild prairie would soon look like: settled farmland. Once white settlers came to the Plains, the buffalo would be killed, the earth fenced off and plowed, and the Indian ways of life gone forever.

By mid-October George was back in St. Louis. He had painted 135 pictures and still felt that this was only the beginning of what he could do. Months in the wilderness had left him more determined than ever to paint the Indians and champion their cause.

Before he left St. Louis, he painted Múk a-tah-mish-o-káh-kaik, Black Hawk. The famous Sac Indian leader was being held prisoner at Jefferson Barracks, a few miles outside of town. The treaty council of 1830, where George had first seen Black Hawk, had failed. Black Hawk, angry that the United States had taken his people's land, had led a group of Sac, Fox, and Kickapoo families east of the Mississippi River into Illinois and Wisconsin. There, federal and state troops, aided by Sioux

In this portrait, the imprisoned leader Black Hawk holds "the skin of a black hawk, from which he had taken his name, and the tail of which made him a fan, which he was almost constantly using."
MÚK-A-TAH-MISH-O-KÁH-KAIK, BLACK HAWK, PROMINENT SAC CHIEF, BY GEORGE CATLIN. SAC AND FOX. OIL, 1832. SMITHSONIAN AMERICAN ART MUSEUM. GIFT OF MRS. JOSEPH HARRISON, JR.

and Menominee fighters, engaged them in a series of battles that became known as the Black Hawk War. Black Hawk's men were defeated, and he and ten other leaders were taken prisoner. The sight of Black Hawk in chains strengthened George's resolve to do what he could to help white people understand and respect the Indian peoples.

Back east, George and Clara were happily reunited. George was glad to learn that many people had read the letters about his trip that had been published in Colonel Stone's newspapers. He and Clara spent a year visiting family and friends. During this time he finished and framed many of his paintings. In Pittsburgh and Louisville he exhibited some of them, and in Cincinnati he lectured about the Indians.

This was the beginning of the second part of George's plan, an idea that had been growing in his mind for the past few years: to put together a grand exhibit of Indian life, his very own traveling museum, that would tour the great cities of the East Coast. But first he had more Indians to paint.

A BALL GAME WITH A THOUSAND PLAYERS

In the spring of 1834 General Henry Leavenworth, Colonel Henry Dodge, four hundred soldiers, and one painter gathered at Fort Gibson, Arkansas Territory. Leavenworth, a hero of the War of 1812, was one of the most important officers on the western frontier. Dodge was a veteran of the Black Hawk War and would soon become governor of the Wisconsin Territory. Their mission: to ride southwest and make contact with the Wichita and Comanche tribes. The U.S. government wanted to secure the Santa Fe Trail and pave the way for future trade. George wanted to paint the Wichitas and Comanches before the white traders destroyed their way of life.

Each company of soldiers had horses of a different color: bay, black, white, sorrel, gray, and cream. To George's eye, it was a pleasing effect, though he worried that the regiment of dragoons (soldiers who traveled on horseback but were trained to fight on foot) might look war-like to the Indians.

While he waited for the expedition to begin, George bought a cream-colored mustang named Charley and rode out to paint the Osage, Cherokee, Choctaw, and Creek Indians who lived on the rolling plains near the fort and on the banks of the Arkansas River. The Osage men sported shaved heads and topknots, and from their pierced ears hung "great quantities of wampum and tinsel ornaments." They were the tallest Indians George had ever seen—many of the men were more than six and a half feet tall. The Osages were native to the area and still lived by hunting. The Cherokees, Choctaws, and Creeks were farmers who had recently been forced to move to this region from their homes back east.

The Choctaws played a ball game similar to lacrosse, on a field two and half times as big as a football field. According to George, the night before a game there was always a "ball-play dance," accompanied by drums. The men danced around their team's goalpost, rattling their "ball-sticks" and singing at the top of their lungs, while the women danced and chanted on the line between the two teams. At the same time, four elderly medicine men, the judges, sat in the middle of the field and smoked a pipe in honor of the Great Spirit. The dance was repeated every half hour, all night.

The game itself might last all day. As

Painted at Fort Gibson, the champion ballplayer Tul-lock-chísh-ko holds "ball-sticks" made of hickory wood and rawhide.
TUL-LOCK-CHÍSH-KO, DRINKS THE JUICE OF THE STONE, IN BALL-PLAYER'S DRESS, BY GEORGE CATLIN. CHOCTAW. OIL, 1834. SMITHSONIAN AMERICAN ART MUSEUM. GIFT OF MRS. JOSEPH HARRISON, JR

many as a thousand men played at once, barefoot and each dressed only in a breechcloth, a beaded belt, a "tail" made of white horsehair or quills, and a "mane" of dyed horsehair.

George watched the games while sitting on Charley. From his high perch he had a good view over the heads of the five thousand other spectators. He didn't want to miss any of the "tricks, and kicks and scuffles" or the "almost superhuman struggles for the ball."

George painted several versions of the Choctaw ball game. This one was created more than ten years after his visit to Fort Gibson.
BALL-PLAY OF THE CHOCTAW—BALL UP, BY GEORGE CATLIN. OIL, 1845–48. SMITHSONIAN AMERICAN ART MUSEUM. GIFT OF MRS. JOSEPH HARRISON, JR.

Hundreds are running together and leaping, actually over each other's heads, and darting between their adversaries' legs, tripping and throwing, and foiling each other in every possible manner, and every voice raised to the highest key, in shrill yelps and barks! . . .

There are times, when the ball gets to the ground, and such a confused mass rushing together around it, and knocking their sticks together . . . when the condensed mass of ball-sticks, and shins, and bloody noses, is carried around the different parts of the ground, for a quarter of an hour at a time, without any one of the mass being able to see the ball.

By June George had had enough of ball games. The expedition into the Southwest was ready to begin. George had met a friend from St. Louis, Joe Chadwick, who would come along. They hoped the tribes would be friendly.

FEVER

General Leavenworth and Colonel Dodge gave the order, and the regiment rode out. In the first ten days they traveled two hundred miles to the Red River, on the Texas-Oklahoma border, past acres of wild plum trees, roses, currants, gooseberries, and prickly pear cacti. The ridges of the prairie were crowned with oaks and wild grape vines.

As they rode farther south and west, trees and shade became hard to find. It was hot under the blinding sun, and water was scarce.

"Sometimes for the distance of many miles, the only water we could find, was in stagnant pools, in which the buffalo have been lying and wallowing like hogs in a mud-puddle," George wrote.

Soon half the regiment fell ill with a "bilious fever," probably from drinking the dirty water. The sick men stayed behind with General

Leavenworth. George and Joe continued west into Comanche territory with the other half of the regiment, under Colonel Dodge's command. No one knew if the Comanches would be hostile or not, but everyone knew of their reputation as fierce fighters.

A few days later, Dodge's men sighted a group of Comanches in the distance. The soldiers formed a line and waited, tense in their saddles. The Comanches rode closer. George gripped Charley's reins, his gun close at hand.

Colonel Dodge ordered a soldier to approach the Indians with a white flag. From the other direction, a Comanche man on a white horse rode toward the soldier.

"The warrior's quiver was slung on the warrior's back, and his bow grasped in his left hand, ready for instant use," George wrote. ". . . His shield was on his arm, and across his thigh, in a beautiful cover of buckskin, his gun was slung—and in his right hand he had a lance of fourteen feet in length."

On the point of the Indian's lance was a piece of white buffalo skin, the Indian version of the white flag of peace. George breathed a sigh of relief. The Comanches were not going to attack.

"They had every reason to look upon us as their natural enemy," he wrote, ". . . and yet they galloped out . . . to shake us by the hand, on the bare assertion of Colonel Dodge . . . that 'we came to see them on a friendly visit.'"

The men on both sides dismounted and smoked a ceremonial pipe. Then they all rode back together to the Comanche village, where George pulled out his paints and got to work. Among the portraits he painted over the next few weeks were His-oo-sán-chees, Little Spaniard (the brave man who had first ridden out to meet the regiment), and Ta-wáh-que-nah, Mountain of Rocks. He also painted some Wichitas, Kiowas, and Wacos, who were friendly with the Comanches. George later described his painting of His-oo-sán-chees in this way:

I have here represented him as he stood for me, with his shield on his arm, with his quiver slung, and his lance of fourteen feet in length in his right hand. This extraordinary little man, whose figure was light, seemed to be all bone and muscle and exhibited immense power. . . . We had many exhibitions of his extraordinary strength, as well as agility; and of his gentlemanly politeness and friendship, we had as frequent evidences.

George was amazed by the Comanches' horsemanship. While carrying a lance, bow, and shield, a Comanche rider could drop down to the side of his horse and hang there at a full gallop, shooting arrows. George loved watching the Comanches show off their skills. Unfortunately, he wasn't able to watch for long. More and more of the soldiers were coming down with the fever, and soon George also became sick. Too weak to travel, he had to stay behind when Joe and some of the soldiers visited the Wichita Indians, ninety miles to the west.

By the time the soldiers returned two weeks later, George was so ill that he could barely sit in his saddle. All around him men were dying. Colonel Dodge ordered the company back to Fort Gibson. George went with them, struggling along on Charley. In six days they reached the other half of the regiment. General Leavenworth was dead, along with ten or fifteen others.

Because His-oo-sán-chees was half Spanish and half Comanche, he was constantly having to prove himself to his tribe by undertaking dangerous tasks, such as being the first to greet the regiment of soldiers. Here he wears a breechcloth and leggings. His long braids are tied with red cloth.
HIS-OO-SÁN-CHEES, LITTLE SPANIARD, A WARRIOR, BY GEORGE CATLIN. COMANCHE/NIUAM. OIL, 1834. SMITHSONIAN AMERICAN ART MUSEUM. GIFT OF MRS. JOSEPH HARRISON, JR.

This picture shows how a Comanche could use his horse as a shield. The Comanches, George wrote, were "the most extraordinary horsemen that I have seen yet in all my travels, and I doubt very much whether any people in the world can surpass them."

COMANCHE FEATS OF HORSEMANSHIP, BY GEORGE CATLIN. COMANCHE/NIUAM. OIL, 1834–35.
SMITHSONIAN AMERICAN ART MUSEUM. GIFT OF MRS. JOSEPH HARRISON, JR.

Now George was too sick to ride. Delirious with fever, he was loaded into an empty wagon and taken back to Fort Gibson. For weeks he lay in bed as funeral processions went by under his window. Would he ever again see his beloved Clara, his parents, his brothers and sisters? He was sure his funeral would be next.

But it wasn't George's time to die. He began to recover. As soon as he could stand up, he decided to leave Fort Gibson. He would ride east, alone, without a map, five hundred miles across the uncharted prairie. At the end of the journey lay the promise of a reunion with Clara.

George asked Joe to ship his paintings by boat to St. Louis. Then, "one fine morning," he wrote,

> *Charley was brought up and saddled, and a bear-skin and a buffalo robe being spread upon his saddle, and a coffee-pot and tin cup tied to it also—with a few pounds of hard biscuit . . . my pistols in my belt—with my sketch-book slung on my back, and a small pocket compass in my pocket; I took leave of Ft. Gibson. . . .*
>
> *No one can imagine what was the dread I felt for that place; nor the pleasure . . . when Charley was trembling under me, and I turned him around on the top of a prairie bluff at a mile distance [from the fort], to take a last look upon it, and thank God . . . that I was not to be buried there. I said to myself that "to die on the prairie, and be devoured by wolves, or to fall in combat and be scalped by an Indian, would be far more acceptable." . . .*
>
> *Day by day I thus pranced and galloped along . . . through waving grass and green fields, occasionally dismounting and lying in the grass an hour or so, until the grim shaking and chattering of an ague chill had passed off; and through the nights, [I] slept on my bear-skin . . . with my saddle for my pillow, and my buffalo robe drawn over me for my covering.*

George and his horse Charley making their way across the prairie.
MY HORSE "CHARLEY" AND I, BY GEORGE CATLIN. ENGRAVING, 1841. FROM CATLIN, LETTERS AND NOTES.

My horse Charley was picketed near me at the end of his laso [sic], which gave him room for his grazing. . . . Gangs of sneaking wolves [sniffed at] our little encampment, [but were] a safe distance from us at sun-rise in the morning—gazing at us, and impatient to pick up the crumbs and bones that were left, when we moved away from our feeble fire that had faintly flickered through the night, and in the absence of timber, had been made of dried buffalo dung.

A month later, George arrived in Boonville, on the Missouri River some 150 miles west of St. Louis. From there he traveled by boat to Alton, Illinois, where he met Clara, whom he hadn't seen for a year. The reunion must have been particularly sweet after his close brush with death. Together they took a steamboat to New Orleans and then went to Pensacola, Florida, where they stayed at the home of George's younger brother James. Another of his younger brothers, Richard, also lived in Pensacola, and George spent time with his family as he recovered his strength. But his adventures among the Indians were not over yet.

THE PIPESTONE QUARRY

After hearing so many of her husband's stories and being apart from him for so long, Clara wanted to see a little bit of the frontier for herself. The following year, at her suggestion, the two of them traveled up the Mississippi River from New Orleans all the way to Fort Snelling, in present-day Minnesota, where George painted Ojibwa and Eastern Sioux (Dakota) Indians. The Mississippi was already a well-established route, with many towns along the way, so this was not a dangerous trip into unexplored territory. George was very protective of his city-bred wife and felt she would be safe.

Partway through the trip, Clara became pregnant with their first child. She boarded a St. Louis–bound steamer in Fort Snelling, while George paddled nine hundred miles of the way back by canoe. He also made a side trip into Iowa to paint the Sac and Fox chief Kee-o-kúk, The Watchful Fox, and his favorite wife.

From St. Louis George shipped his collection of paintings and Indian articles to Buffalo, New York, where he planned to earn some money by exhibiting them. He and Clara returned east, and their baby

In this painting done at Fort Snelling in 1835, Jú-ah-kís-gaw wears a dress of factory-made cloth "decorated and ornamented according to Indian taste." She carries her baby in a traditional Ojibwa cradle. George wrote that cradles were used until babies were about six months old, after which they were carried on their mothers' backs.

JÚ-AH-KÍS-GAW, WOMAN WITH HER CHILD IN A CRADLE, BY GEORGE CATLIN. OJIBWA (CHIPPEWA). OIL, 1835. SMITHSONIAN AMERICAN ART MUSEUM. GIFT OF MRS. JOSEPH HARRISON, JR.

MAP TK

was born in Albany in the spring of 1836. Unfortunately, the baby lived only five days. Although infant death was common at the time, George and Clara were heartbroken.

Still, George felt the show had to go on. He left his grieving wife with her family and went to Buffalo, where his father and two of his brothers, Henry and Francis, helped prepare the exhibit. A hall was rented, the paintings were hung, and advertisements were printed, when suddenly George announced he was leaving. There was only one boat that year heading to Sault Sainte Marie (in present-day Michigan), and George had decided that he had to be on it. He wanted to see the sacred stone quarry from which many of the Plains Indians got the special red stone for their ceremonial pipes.

George's sudden decision caught everyone by surprise. His thinking was that this might be his last chance to visit the quarry before devoting himself completely to his Indian exhibit. He was about to turn forty, and soon he and Clara would try again to start a family. Once they had children, it would be harder for him to go off on dangerous adventures for months at a time. And with family responsibilities would come the need for more income, which he hoped the exhibit would provide.

George told his father and brothers to pack up the paintings and put them in storage until he returned. They were dismayed and tried to talk him out of it. Father pleaded with him not to go. Mother thought he was crazy. But George had always been headstrong and quick to act on a whim, especially when it involved Indians and adventure. His mind was made up. In July he set out for the red pipestone quarry.

George's journey took him several thousand miles across the Great Lakes to Detroit, Sault Sainte Marie, Mackinaw, and Green Bay, then by river and over land to Prairie du Chien, Wisconsin Territory, and across present-day Minnesota. On the last leg of the trip, he was joined by Robert Serrill Wood, an Englishman he met in Green Bay.

George's interests in geology and Indian cultures came together at the pipestone quarry.

PIPESTONE QUARRY ON THE COTEAU DES PRAIRIES, BY GEORGE CATLIN. OIL, 1836–37. SMITHSONIAN AMERICAN ART MUSEUM. GIFT OF MRS. JOSEPH HARRISON, JR.

The quarry was sacred to many tribes. Any white man who was discovered there might be put to death. But that didn't stop George. One hundred fifty miles from the quarry, according to George, he and Robert were surrounded by Sioux Indians. The Sioux thought that George and Robert had been sent by the United States government to find out how much the quarry was worth. Years later, George recalled what they said to him:

"The white people," said one, "when they see anything in our country that they want, send officers to value it, and then if they can't buy it, they will get it some other way. . . .

"We know that the whites are like a great cloud that rises in the East, and will cover the whole country. We know that they will have all our lands; but if ever they get our Red Pipe Quarry they will have to pay very dear for it."

George told them he hadn't been sent by the government but was traveling only to satisfy his own curiosity. The Sioux were still suspicious. The red stone was "part of their flesh," they said, and if a white man touched it, "a hole would be made in their flesh, and the blood could never be made to stop running."

Robert wanted to turn back. But George told the Indians, "We have heard that the Red Pipe Quarry was a great curiosity, and we have started to go to it, and we will not be stopped."

According to George, the Sioux were finally convinced and let them pass.

A few days later George and Robert found the quarry on a plateau called the Coteau des Prairies, in what is now southwestern Minnesota. As he gazed at this sacred place, George was filled with awe. Many Plains tribes believed the quarry was a gift from the Great Spirit and had used its rock since time beyond memory. Here, bitter enemies would put aside their weapons and work side by side in peace.

George painted several pictures of the quarry and broke with sacred Indian tradition by taking a small sample of rock, which he later sent to a famous mineralogist in Boston. The scientist declared it to be a previously unknown mineral compound, and named it catlinite.

The bowl and stem of a Plains Indian pipe are two separate pieces. The bowl of this pipe is catlinite. The stem is carved wood, decorated with porcupine quills.
PHOTOGRAPH COURTESY KANSAS STATE HISTORICAL SOCIETY.

George knew it was disrespectful to visit the sacred quarry against the wishes of the Indians. His behavior was unusual for a man who claimed to honor the Indian ways. But for some reason he felt he had to see the quarry, no matter what. He was lucky to survive the visit.

While he was traveling in the wilderness, George was out of touch with family and friends for several months, longer than at any time in the past. They didn't hear from him and feared the worst. It was particularly hard on Clara, who wrote to George's mother that she was afraid she might never see him again. In November, George's brother Henry finally received a letter that had been posted in Tecumseh, southwest of Detroit. George was on his way home, and he had big plans. It was time to show his paintings to the world.

PART THREE

The Showman, 1837–54

~~~

THE TALK OF THE TOWN

On September 25, 1837, George Catlin's "Indian Gallery" opened at Clinton Hall in New York City. In it were five hundred paintings and thousands of Indian artifacts. Some of the artifacts had been given to him as gifts. For others he had traded beads, trinkets, and various items the Indians had wanted. Included in the exhibit were buffalo robes, shirts, belts, moccasins, lances, spears, shields, war clubs, bows, whistles, rattles, drums, necklaces, wampum (shell beads strung into patterned belts for ceremonial use and exchange), pipes, medicine bags, headdresses, and a complete Crow tipi. Admission was fifty cents, about ten dollars in today's money.

New Yorkers had never seen anything like the Indian Gallery. Popular entertainment at the time consisted of concerts, plays, or perhaps a visit to Peale's Museum and Gallery of Fine Arts, founded by Rubens Peale. There one could listen to a band play "Yankee Doodle," gawk at a stuffed rhinoceros, or watch a fourteen-foot-long anaconda swallow a live hen. Pictures of Plains Indians and the West were something new. The citizens of New York flocked to George's Gallery.

Every evening George stood in the hall and lectured about the exhibit. People came expecting to hear about bloody massacres. Instead, George spoke about the Indians' sense of honor. Through his stories he tried to convince white audiences that Indians were intelligent people worthy of respect, who fought against the whites only because their land was being taken from them.

George knew how to spin a tale and, at forty-one, he was a well-spoken and distinguished-looking man. Still, some people didn't believe his stories. How could he have painted so many tribes in such a short time? How could he have traveled so far into Indian territory and not been scalped? How could a "mere Indian" like Kee-o-kúk own so fine a horse?

As newspapers began to write about the show, the crowds grew. By November, George had moved the Gallery to a larger hall and raised the admission price to a dollar. Word got out that Kee-o-kúk was in New York and planned to visit the Gallery with his wife and twenty tribesmen. George sold 1,500 tickets at twice the usual price. Kee-o-kúk told the audience that he did indeed own the splendid horse in George's picture.

George's father saw the exhibit and wrote to George's youngest brother, Francis, "You can hardly imagine the splendor of his Gallery as exhibited in

Kee-o-kúk was Black Hawk's rival for leadership of the Sac and Fox people. Black Hawk fought against the U.S. government, whereas Kee-o-kúk thought it wiser to sign treaties. In the end, neither man was able to prevent the loss of Sac and Fox land.

George honored Kee-o-kúk by painting him on horseback, a pose often used in monumental sculptures of generals and kings.

KEE-O-KÚK, THE WATCHFUL FOX, CHIEF OF THE TRIBE, ON HORSEBACK, BY GEORGE CATLIN. SAC AND FOX. OIL, 1835. SMITHSONIAN AMERICAN ART MUSEUM. GIFT OF MRS. JOSEPH HARRISON, JR.

One of George's most famous pictures, this painting sums up his feelings about the sad fate that awaited Indians once they were exposed to white civilization. After Wi-jún-jon visited Washington and told his fellow villagers what he had seen, they found his stories so unbelievable that they branded him a liar. He sank into disgrace and was eventually killed because he was believed to be working with evil spirits.

WI-JÚN-JON, PIGEON'S EGG HEAD (THE LIGHT), GOING TO AND RETURNING FROM WASHINGTON, BY GEORGE CATLIN. ASSINIBOINE/NAKODA. OIL, 1837–39. SMITHSONIAN AMERICAN ART MUSEUM. GIFT OF MRS. JOSEPH HARRISON, JR.

N. York. . . . I have never been acquainted with a man more popular than he is among all classes."

George was thrilled, and his happiness grew in December when Clara gave birth to a healthy baby girl. Her name was Elizabeth, and they called her Libby.

A month later George closed the Indian Gallery for a few weeks and went to South Carolina to paint Os-ce-o-lá. The famous Seminole leader from Florida had been betrayed by the U.S. government and was being held prisoner at Fort Moultrie.

"This gallant fellow," George wrote, ". . . [was] sent to this place for safe-keeping, where he is grieving with a broken spirit, and ready to die, cursing white man, no doubt, to the end of his breath."

Os-ce-o-lá died of an infection a few days after George painted him. When George returned to New York and reopened the Gallery, the new portrait attracted a lot of attention.

In April 1838 George moved the Indian Gallery to Washington, D.C. While there, he tried to convince the government to buy his collection and make it part of a new national museum. He also asked Congress to set aside land out west, in a kind of "national park," where the buffalo would be protected from the fur companies and the Indians could live in their traditional ways. George's national-park concept was different from what eventually became the system of Indian reservations. Reservations were not necessarily located on ancestral land, and the residents were usually expected to take up farming, to stop speaking their native language, and to convert to Christianity.

George had powerful friends in Congress, and the government did consider buying his collection. But in the end Congress took no action. Too many politicians were unsympathetic to the Indians. It didn't help that in his lectures George criticized the government and its support for the fur companies. He felt that many laws were unfair to the Indians and wasn't afraid to say so. It would be eight years before Congress authorized a national museum—and the first national park would not be created until 1872. Neither was anything like what George had in mind.

Over the next few months, with the help of an assistant named Daniel Kavanaugh, George took the Indian Gallery to Baltimore, Philadelphia, and Boston. In all three cities it was a big hit. Clara and baby Libby stayed for the summer in Utica, New York, with George's favorite sister, Eliza, then joined him in Boston.

In the spring of 1839 the Gallery reopened in New York and then had a second run in Philadelphia. During this time George continued to try to sell his collection to Congress. Sixty thousand dollars (about $1.2 million in today's money) was a reasonable price, he thought, for what many people were calling a national treasure.

LEFT: George distributed leaflets like this one in every city in which he exhibited the Indian Gallery. BROADSIDE ADVERTISING "CATLIN'S INDIAN GALLERY," WASHINGTON, D.C., APRIL 1838. LIBRARY OF CONGRESS.

RIGHT: Each portrait in the Indian Gallery came with a certificate signed by witnesses. George wanted to prove that his subjects were who he said they were and that he had painted them on the frontier. CERTIFICATE OF AUTHENTICITY. IMAGE COURTESY OF GEORGE CATLIN PAPERS, 1821–1904 & 1946, IN THE ARCHIVES OF AMERICAN ART, SMITHSONIAN INSTITUTION.

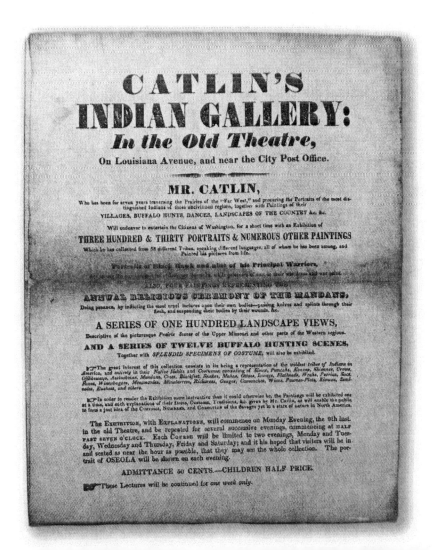

But Congress didn't budge, and so George announced that he was taking the Gallery to London, the capital of England. If the American government didn't want his collection, perhaps the English government would.

George thought the politicians in Washington would change their minds when they heard that his collection was leaving the country. Newspaper editorials urged Congress to take action. They said the Gallery should belong to the American people and that it would be a disgrace if a foreign government bought it.

It was a stressful time for George. He was a natural showman and was making a lot of money, but his expenses were huge. It cost him a fortune to ship eight tons of paintings and artifacts from city to city, and in each city he had to print programs, buy advertisements in the newspapers, and pay rent for a hall. For the show in Washington alone he printed 2,500 catalogs and 10,850 leaflets. Despite the Gallery's popularity, he was barely able to pay his bills.

Father wrote that he wished George could "settle down . . . & finish his books of travels and have a comfortable home." If Congress had bought the Indian Gallery, perhaps George would have settled down. Instead, the government made no offer, and so in the fall of 1839 he packed his collection into crates, loaded them aboard a ship bound for England, and set out across the ocean in search of fame and fortune.

Clara was pregnant again and would join him later. With him went his assistant, Daniel; his twenty-one-year-old nephew, Theodore Burr (the son of George's oldest brother, Charles); and two live grizzly bear cubs, chained in a cage on the deck.

THE INDIAN GALLERY TAKES LONDON BY STORM

Through the bustling streets of the grand and ancient city of London, George made his way. He rented expensive rooms to live in, "central, extravagant & fashionable—& only ones in the city that would do." He signed a lease for an exhibit hall with a room 106 feet long. He bought advertisements in fifty-one newspapers. He had leaflets printed:

CATLIN'S GALLERY
OF
NORTH AMERICAN INDIANS
EGYPTIAN HALL, PICCADILLY

An English friend introduced him to lords and ladies, each of whom got a special invitation to the exhibit. With Burr and Daniel's help, George unpacked the crates and set up the Gallery. He had hoped to exhibit the grizzly bears, but the wild animals proved too hard to handle. They were sent to the zoo for safekeeping.

George was dazzled by the wealthy Londoners in their fancy carriages, by the imposing royal palaces and stately townhouses, by the crowds in the streets and the many boats and barges that plied the river Thames. London was the largest city he had ever seen; with some two million inhabitants, it was the largest in the world. In comparison, New York's population was a mere 312,000.

Egyptian Hall, at 22 Piccadilly Street, can be seen in the right foreground of this print. The rent was 550 British pounds a year—about $55,000 in today's money.
PICCADILLY, LOOKING TOWARDS THE CITY, BY THOMAS SHOTTER BOYS. LITHOGRAPH, 1842. FROM BOYS, *ORIGINAL VIEWS OF LONDON AS IT IS. . . .* LONDON: T. BOYS, 1842.

In his letters, George never mentioned London's vast slums or the hordes of children laboring in filthy factories, probably because they were tucked away in parts of the city he never saw. But he did notice the beggars in the streets and always gave them pennies as he walked by.

As the grand opening of the Gallery approached, George worried about whether the exhibit would be a success.

"I am now in the midst of strangers and in a few days to make my bow to the Lords & Ladies—," he wrote to his parents, "and in the midst of confusion and difficulties of arranging, and hanging, &c &c, you can well imagine something of my anxieties."

He was also waiting for news from Clara about the new baby. He missed his wife and was worried about her because childbirth was dangerous in those days.

"The suspense is painful to me at this critical time, beyond what I can possibly describe," he wrote.

By the end of January the Gallery was ready. For three days George held a "private viewing" for the cream of London society. Standing next to his paintings, he welcomed dukes and duchesses, earls and countesses, lords and baronets, knights and bishops, and assorted "literary and scientific gentlemen." Then he opened the Gallery to the public. Admission: one shilling (about five dollars in today's money).

George's show created a sensation. He became a celebrity overnight.

The next few months were thrilling and exhausting. All day long George answered questions at the exhibit hall. Three nights a week he gave a formal lecture, after which he was wined and dined by the nobility.

Everyone wanted to hear stories about his adventures among the Indians. Londoners did not share white Americans' prejudice against Indians, who were far away across the ocean and therefore posed no threat. Instead, the Indians were exotic objects of fascination.

The English had read about Indians in novels and had formed romantic notions about them—notions that were far from reality. They imagined the American West to be a place of unlimited bounty and endless thrills. Listening to George, they could almost feel the wind whistling through the prairie grass and hear the thundering stampede of the buffalo.

George loved the attention and threw himself into the social whirlwind.

"You will all rejoice to hear that I am well, although almost half crazy with the bustle and excitement," he wrote to his parents. He admired the elegant Londoners and worried that he was just "a green horn from the backwoods." But, he added, "I have kept as cool as possible—have pursued steadily & unflinchingly my course, and have at last succeeded in making what they call here, a *decided hit.*"

By now George had received news that the new baby had been born. He was overjoyed. They had agreed to name her Clara Gregory Catlin and called her Conny. George couldn't wait to see Clara and the girls and quickly sent money so that they could join him in London. "When they arrive . . . it will be the happiest moment of my life," he wrote. He hoped that his father would also come and was disappointed when Father said he was too old to make the trip.

For her part, Clara was sorry to leave her elderly parents, but she knew that her place was at her husband's side. George's excitement was contagious, and she believed in him, in his talent, and in his ability to secure for them a comfortable life. If his plans required her to cross an ocean and raise her children far from friends and family, so be it.

The day of Clara's arrival, George and Burr went down to the dock. George watched the ship approach "with throbbing heart . . . until she came so near that I recognized amid the throng on her deck, the well known face of my fair & dear little Clara & Libby lifted in her arms. . . . I at length caught her eye & waved my hat, and in a moment was on board, with Burr at my side! I cannot possibly express to you the gush of pleasure of that moment."

George and Burr tucked Clara, Libby, baby Conny, and their nursemaid into a carriage and took them back to George's rented rooms. George couldn't wait to show Clara the city and introduce her to his new friends. Within a few days he began to whisk her around London. His friends arranged for special visits inside royal palaces and a peek at wheelbarrows full of gold at the mint. George and Clara, dressed in Indian costumes from the Gallery, even went to a masquerade ball and won a prize.

For several weeks the partying continued. Then summer arrived and with it the "dull season," during which fashionable Londoners fled to the countryside. Fewer people came to see the Gallery, and George worried that he would run out of money. Clara was concerned, too.

George's nephew Burr was one of the men who performed in the Indian Gallery.
Theodore Burr Catlin, in Indian Costume, by George Catlin. Oil, 1840–41. Smithsonian American Art Museum. Gift of Mrs. Joseph Harrison, Jr.

Both of them knew that people who didn't pay their bills in England were thrown into debtors' prison, a practice that had already been abolished in much of the United States.

"We are here in a strange land struggling for a living," Clara wrote to George's parents, "and if a man is unfortunate here, there is a set of harpies ready to pounce upon him, and take all he has."

George worried about the lack of visitors but kept the Gallery open. He had a surprise in store for the fall.

When Londoners returned to town, there was an exciting new attraction at the Indian Gallery. George had hired twenty local men and boys, dressed them in Indian costumes and war paint, and trained them to perform Indian songs and dances. Every night they stamped and whooped their way through the hall. Londoners loved it, and business picked up. George heard that the British Museum might make an offer to buy his collection. There was even a rumor that Queen Victoria might visit.

George was so busy that Clara and the girls sometimes saw him only late at night. Still, Clara wrote, "Our little daughters are fat and hearty, and George feels very happy when he comes home at night, and gets one on each knee."

Some 32,500 people came to see the Indian Gallery that first year. George made more than $9,000—about $180,000 in today's money—and he spent every penny.

Life in London was expensive. George had rent to pay, as well as salaries for the performers. He had a family to support—a family that was still growing, for in the summer of 1841 the Catlins had a third daughter, Louise Victoria. Meanwhile, his parents were getting old, and he wished he could send them more money.

The financial pressures on George were constant and unrelenting. He was already beginning to feel bitter that Congress had not bought the Gallery. He must have sometimes wished to be back among the Indians, where life had seemed so simple.

"I would gladly retire from the bustle & bother of the business world, of which I am completely sick," he wrote.

But this was just wishful thinking. George couldn't retire. He needed money and would just have to figure out a way to make it. The answer, he thought, was to write a book.

Queen Victoria reigned for sixty-three years. She is shown here with seven of her nine children.

VICTORIA, QUEEN OF GREAT BRITAIN AND IRELAND, 1819–1901. PHOTOGRAVURE BY BOUSSOD VALADON & CO. AFTER AN ORIGINAL PAINTING BY JOHN PHILIP, CA. 1897. LIBRARY OF CONGRESS.

OJIBWAS AND IOWAS ONSTAGE

In October 1841 George published an eight-hundred-page book with illustrations based on his paintings. *Letters and Notes on the Manners, Customs, and Condition of the North American Indians, Written During Eight Years' Travel Amongst the Wildest Tribes of Indians of North America (1832–1839)* got rave reviews. It sold more than twenty thousand copies, far more than any other book about the North American Indians at that time. Now George was as famous for his writing as for his painting.

Unfortunately, the book cost so much to print and sell that he made very little profit. He had to find another way to earn money for his family. They were depending on him.

George treasured Clara and doted on his little girls. No matter how far he traveled or for how long, Clara provided a home to which he could always return. She gave his heart a resting place, too. In his letters to her he shared anxieties and doubts that he shared with no one else.

George decided to move the family to a small house in the suburbs of London and take his show on the road. He exhibited the Gallery in Liverpool, about two hundred miles northwest of London, then toured with his performers to other cities in northern England, Scotland, and Ireland. When the tour was over, George and Clara agreed it was time to go home to the United States.

Just as they were about to leave, a Canadian named Arthur Rankin arrived in England with a group of Ojibwa Indians, all men. Rankin had hired the Indians and was planning to set up a show featuring them. People told him he would succeed only if he worked with George. George didn't trust Rankin, but since the Ojibwas were already in England, George agreed to team up with him. As a friend to all Indians, George said, he wanted to make sure the Ojibwas' trip was worth their while and that they didn't get into any trouble. It was also a financial opportunity George could not resist. He reopened the Gallery in London, and the Ojibwas danced as part of the exhibit.

For a while the presence of real Indians brought in new audiences. George and the Ojibwas were even invited to Windsor Castle to perform for the queen. But some people criticized George for putting live Indians in his show. They said he was selfishly using the Indians for his own gain.

In the end it turned out that George shouldn't have trusted Arthur

Rankin. They got into an argument, after which Rankin decided to open his own show with the Ojibwas, competing with George. Rankin's show lured audiences away from the Indian Gallery.

At around the same time, Clara learned that her father had died, and a few days later George heard that his father, Putnam, had died, too. He felt terrible that he hadn't been with him at the end of his life. He hoped that his brother Francis might visit England with his family, but Francis was busy settling Putnam's estate. For Clara, who already bore the burden of caring for the children without the comfort and help of close friends and family, the loss was even greater. The ocean separating them from home seemed wide, indeed.

Discouraged, George closed the Gallery and went to the country to work on another book. He promised Clara that they would go back to America as soon as it was finished. She had just had another child and was anxious to return home. The new baby was a boy, George Catlin, Jr.

In 1844 George published *Catlin's North American Indian Portfolio: Hunting Scenes and Amusements of the Rocky Mountains and Prairies of America*. It was shorter than his first book, but the illustrations were more beautiful, and it sold well. Clara wrote to George's mother that they might be home in the fall.

The woman with the long shawl at the far left of the picture is Queen Victoria. Next to her is her husband, Prince Albert. George gestures toward the dancers.

Ojibwa Dancing Before Queen Victoria, by George Catlin. Engraving, 1848. From Catlin, Catlin's Notes of Eight Years' Travels and Residence in Europe.

George later wrote that just as they were about to leave, a white man named George H. C. Melody arrived in London with fourteen Iowa Indians. In fact, Melody worked for the American showman P. T. Barnum, and George had probably already struck a deal with Barnum to bring the group from the United States.

Barnum was producing several shows in London that year. His most famous performer was Charles Sherwood Stratton, a dapper little person whose stage name was General Tom Thumb. Stratton had been singing and dancing in another exhibition room in the same hall where George's paintings were on exhibit. The two showmen agreed to work together, but Barnum had no interest in the welfare of Indians. He wanted only to make money. George considered him "a low and contemptible fellow," which is probably why George left him out of his later version of events.

The group of Iowas included men, women, and several children. There was even a baby named Corsair, the son of Shon-ta-yi-ga, Little Wolf, and O-kee-wee-me, Female Bear That Walks on the Back of Another. Leading the delegation were Mew-hew-she-kaw, White Cloud, a chief, and See-non-ty-ya, Blistered Feet, a medicine man.

George knew some of the Iowa men from the frontier and loved the idea of being among Indians again. He hired the whole group to perform songs, dances, and ceremonies, rehung his show, and reopened for business in London. Clara reluctantly agreed to postpone the family's return to America.

Once again George and his Indian Gallery were the talk of the town. The prime minister invited George and the Iowas to lunch. See-non-ty-ya spent all morning painting his face and body and checking his appearance in a small looking glass that hung from his belt.

From the moment George had first arrived in England, people there had been curious about American Indians. His exhibits, lectures, books, and shows changed many people's impressions of Indians. At the same time, the Indians who worked with George were interested in

Charles Sherwood Stratton was about two and a half feet tall when this daguerreotype (an early kind of photograph) was made. He continued to grow throughout his life and was three feet four inches tall when he died.

P.T. Barnum and General Tom Thumb, by Samuel Root and Marcus Aurelius Root. Daguerreotype, ca. 1850. National Portrait Gallery, Smithsonian Institution.

learning about the English. After the Iowas saw Westminster Abbey and St. Paul's Cathedral, George tried to explain the difference between Catholics, Protestants, and Jews. The Iowas thought it was funny that white people had so many different religions. When George took the Iowas to the zoo, See-non-ty-ya howled in dismay at the sight of a caged wolf. Afterward, the Indians were very quiet. They felt that animals did not belong behind bars.

That winter George took the Iowas to perform in northern England, Scotland, and Ireland while Clara stayed behind in London with Libby, Conny, Louise, and George, Jr. The Iowas were shocked to see so many beggars in the white people's big cities, and to learn that thousands of white men had to work underground in coal mines.

LEFT: Ru-ton-ye-wee-ma was the wife of Mew-hew-she-kaw, White Cloud, the leader of the group of Iowas that arrived in London in 1844. She holds their daughter, Ta-pa-ta-me, Sophia, or Wisdom.
RU-TON-YE-WEE-MA, STRUTTING PIGEON, WIFE OF WHITE CLOUD, BY GEORGE CATLIN. IOWA. OIL, 1844. SMITHSONIAN AMERICAN ART MUSEUM. GIFT OF MRS. JOSEPH HARRISON, JR.

RIGHT: Wash-ka-mon-ya's face and body paint tell the story of his success as a warrior. The handprints indicate victory in hand-to-hand combat.
WASH-KA-MON-YA, FAST DANCER, A WARRIOR, BY GEORGE CATLIN. IOWA. OIL, 1844. SMITHSONIAN AMERICAN ART MUSEUM. GIFT OF MRS. JOSEPH HARRISON, JR.

Although this photograph of Westminster Abbey was taken many years after George and the Iowas visited, the church looks much the same.

WESTMINSTER ABBEY, ENGLAND'S MOST CELEBRATED BUILDING, LONDON. PHOTOGRAPHER UNKNOWN. STEREOGRAPH, CA. 1902, H. C. WHITE CO. LIBRARY OF CONGRESS.

Sadly, on that tour some of the Iowas got sick, and two died. One was Shon-ta-yi-ga and O-kee-wee-me's baby, Corsair. Far from home and unable to perform traditional burial rites, the parents were distraught. They tearfully buried the baby in a Quaker cemetery.

By the time the troupe returned to London, everyone was worn out and ready to go home to America. Clara told George that he had done enough lecturing and should get back to painting.

But George had another idea. He wanted to take his Gallery and the Iowas to Paris, the capital of France. The Iowas had their doubts but agreed to go. George's dutiful wife began to pack the family's belongings once again, in preparation for the move.

Before they left London, an English lord may have offered to buy the Gallery for $35,000 ($700,000 or $800,000 in today's money). If the story is true, George said no. He didn't want his collection hidden away in a castle where no one would see it. He hadn't given up hope that the United States government would buy the Gallery. Besides, he had promised the Iowas that they could meet the king of France.

LOSS

The Catlins and the Iowas arrived in Paris in April 1845. Not long after, King Louis Philippe invited them to perform for the royal family at the Tuileries Palace.

Louis Philippe warmly welcomed his American guests. He had visited the American West as a young man and remembered his time there as one of great happiness. He shared stories about his carefree days floating down the Mississippi River. After the Iowas sang and danced, everyone could see that the king was content. George knew then that the Gallery would be a success in Paris.

The Iowas had a good time in the French capital. They went to parties and a masked ball. They laughed at the Parisians' fancy leather dog leashes, which were decorated with ribbons. They were glad to see a hospital for old soldiers and relieved that there were no beggars in Paris, as there had been in London. Back home in the Iowa villages, where extended families lived together, there was no such thing as a beggar. Among the Iowas the elderly were respected, their wisdom and experience highly valued.

In London the Iowas had also seen dogs leading blind men. When the Indians saw so many women walking dogs in Paris, they assumed that the women were blind. George explained that the dogs were pets. The Indians were surprised. With so many orphanages in Paris, why didn't the thousands of women who had pet dogs each adopt a lost child? To the Iowas, taking care of children came first.

George rented a hall on the Rue St. Honoré and opened his exhibit in June. All of Paris flocked to see it. Important politicians and influential newspaper editors paid visits, as did famous writers Charles Baudelaire, George Sand, and Victor Hugo and painters Eugène Delacroix and Rosa Bonheur. The Catlins settled into their rooms at the Victoria Hotel, and George even found time to paint. He made new friends, among them the Prussian explorer and scientist Baron Alexander von Humboldt, with whom he toured the Louvre Museum.

LEFT: French musician Alex Ropicquet composed two piano pieces in honor of the Iowas' visit to Paris. This print is an advertisement for the music.
LES INDIENS À PARIS. LITHOGRAPH, 1845–46. IMAGE COURTESY OF GEORGE CATLIN PAPERS, 1821–1904 & 1946, IN THE ARCHIVES OF AMERICAN ART, SMITHSONIAN INSTITUTION.

RIGHT: The young French artist Rosa Bonheur (1822–99) was very impressed by the Indian Gallery. Many years later she made a portrait of Colonel William F. "Buffalo Bill" Cody when his Wild West show was visiting Paris. In this fanciful advertisement she is shown painting Buffalo Bill and Napoleon Bonaparte.
BUFFALO BILL'S WILD WEST AND CONGRESS OF ROUGH RIDERS OF THE WORLD. POSTER, CA. 1896. COURIER LITHO. CO., BUFFALO, N.Y. LIBRARY OF CONGRESS.

Unfortunately, the happy days in Paris did not last long. A few weeks after the Indian Gallery opened, two more of the Iowas got sick and died, including O-kee-wee-me, Shon-ta-yi-ga's wife.

"Every day that he afterwards spent in Paris," George wrote, "he ordered a cab to take him to the grave, that he could cry over it, and talk to the departed spirit."

The grief-stricken Iowas decided to return to America. Their sudden departure was a blow to George. But it was nothing compared to what was to come.

As the Iowas were leaving, Clara Catlin was coming down with a cold. Before long she developed pneumonia. There was no medicine for it, and the doctors could do nothing to help her. Within days George's beautiful wife was dead.

GRIEF UPON GRIEF

George closed the Gallery and sent Clara's body back to Brooklyn, New York, to be buried by her family. His faithful Clara had always believed in him. Now she was lost forever. Overwhelmed with grief and guilt, he told himself that her death was his fault. He should have taken his family back to America sooner. He should take the children home now. But what would happen to the Gallery?

He had debts. Responsibilities. Bills to pay. It was up to him to see that the children—ages seven, five, four, and one—were taken care of. He had to keep working, to bring in money. But how? With the Iowas gone, would people still pay to see the Indian Gallery?

Just then a group of eleven Canadian Ojibwa men, women, and children arrived in Paris from England. This was a different group from the one that had worked with Arthur Rankin. George, desperate to support his stricken family, saw a moneymaking opportunity and hired the Ojibwas immediately. In October the new troupe performed for the royal family. The king was so pleased that he let George set up the

Indian Gallery in the Louvre Museum for six weeks. Louis Philippe visited several times and accepted George's offer to make copies of fifteen paintings to hang in his palace at Versailles.

When the exhibit closed, George left his four children with a governess in Paris and took the Ojibwas on a tour to other European cities. It was a disaster. On the first stop eight of the Indians came down with smallpox, and two died. George canceled the tour, sent the Ojibwas back to England, and returned to Paris. The expenses of the tour, hospital bills, and passage to London for the Indians cost George almost $2,000 (about $45,000–$50,000 in today's money).

By now it was winter, and the broad boulevards that had been filled with gaiety and laughter a few months earlier were cold and gray. Sobered by his experiences with the Iowas and Ojibwas and still griev-

This daguerreotype is thought to be a picture of some of the Ojibwas who worked for George in Paris in 1845. If so, the boy on the right is probably Ud-je-jock, Pelican (see front jacket of this book).

PORTRAIT PHOTOGRAPH OF A GROUP OF OJIBWA INDIANS. PHOTOGRAPHER UNKNOWN. DAGUERREOTYPE, CA. 1845. CHICAGO HISTORY MUSEUM; ICHi-08800.

This illustration shows the Indian Gallery as it looked when it was installed in the Louvre Museum. George hung his paintings "salon style," one above the other, and put the Crow tipi in the middle of the room. He is holding open the tipi flap so that people can look inside. The woman and four children on the right may be George's children and their governess.

CATLIN'S COLLECTION IN THE SALLE DE SÉANCE, BY GEORGE CATLIN. ENGRAVING, 1848. FROM CATLIN, *CATLIN'S NOTES OF EIGHT YEARS' TRAVELS AND RESIDENCE IN EUROPE.*

ing for Clara, George stayed home and worked on the fifteen paintings for the king. He was sorry now that he had turned his Indian Gallery into a Wild West show. Far from being "a friend of the Indians," he had used them to make money.

That winter George was very lonely without Clara. But his children were his dearest companions, especially George, Jr., who was two. George loved to watch his son march around the room, banging loudly on a toy drum while the girls played quietly nearby. The girls had been raised to be proper young ladies and tried to behave well for their father's sake. But all the children missed their mother terribly.

George wrote to friends in England and the United States, asking for help in finding someone who would buy the Gallery. He appealed again to Congress, offering the idea that his collection could form the basis of a Museum of Mankind. Meanwhile, he painted. It felt good to have a paintbrush in his hands again. When he was busy painting, he didn't have to think about his money troubles or how much he missed his wife. In his imagination he was back among the Indians.

Over time, the sadness began to lift from George's heart. He saw his friends again and went to parties. When the fifteen paintings were done, the king was pleased and hung them in the palace at Versailles. George didn't know it yet, but the United States Congress was talking about buying the Gallery. Unfortunately, opponents of the purchase pointed out that the government already owned portraits of more than one hundred Indian chiefs, painted by an artist named Charles Bird King. And when war broke out between the United States and Mexico in the spring of 1846, Congress forgot all about George Catlin.

That summer an epidemic of typhoid fever began to rage through Paris. George watched helplessly as first one and then another of his children got sick. Before long, all four were stricken. Once again the doctors could do nothing. The girls pulled through, but not his little drummer boy. George's beloved son died.

As Libby, Conny, and Louise lay in bed recovering, George, Jr.'s tiny body was sent to America to be buried next to Clara's. George was so devastated that two weeks went by before he could find the strength to tell the girls about their brother's death.

"Two idols of my heart had thus vanished," George later wrote, ". . . leaving my breast with a *healing* and a *fresh wound,* to be opened and bleeding together."

In the sad months that followed, George struggled to pay his bills and care for his daughters. He worked on a new series of twenty-seven historical

Before photography was invented, paintings provided a visual record of important people and diplomatic events. Charles Bird King was hired by the federal government to paint portraits of Indians who visited Washington between 1821 and 1842. Tragically, the paintings were lost in a fire at the Smithsonian in 1865.

Nesouaquoit (Bear in the Fork of a Tree). Sac and Fox. Lithograph after an original painting by Charles Bird King, 1837. From McKenney, Thomas L., and James Hall, *History of the Indian Tribes of North America.* Philadelphia: Edward C. Biddle, 1837, vol. 1.

When he was a teenager, Louis Philippe, Duke of Chartres, supported the French Revolution. But revolutionary leaders became politically extreme, and in 1793 the young duke was forced into exile. He returned to France after the fall of Napoleon in 1815 and was proclaimed King of the French in 1830, a title he held until the Revolution of 1848.

LOUIS-PHILIPPE, ROI DES FRANÇAIS, 1841. FROM LA REINE VICTORIA D'APRÈS SA CORRESPONDENCE INÉDITE. . . . PARIS: HACHETTE, 1907. (PHOTO Y. A. DURELLE-MARC.)

paintings that he later said the king had commissioned. It is more likely that the king had shown interest but had never promised to buy them.

Back in Washington, D.C., Congress once again considered purchasing the Indian Gallery. An amendment was introduced, suggesting that the newly created Smithsonian Institution take charge of the Indian Gallery. But Joseph Henry, the director of the Smithsonian, felt that its main purpose was research, not running museums or art galleries. A senator from Florida, remembering George's sympathetic painting of the Seminole leader Os-ce-o-lá, said it would be more fitting for the government to spend money on paintings of the white people murdered by Indians. The amendment was defeated.

George worked on King Louis Philippe's paintings for almost a year and delivered them to the Louvre in early 1848. Louis Philippe was to view them there and, George hoped, decide to purchase them. George thought he would earn at least $3,000 (more than $60,000 in today's money).

But a revolution was brewing in Paris. Mobs swarmed through the streets. With the last of his money George packed up the Gallery and fled to England with his daughters. Days later, rebels seized the king's throne. George hadn't been paid a cent for his twenty-seven paintings.

BANKRUPT

The next few years were dark ones for George Catlin. He opened an exhibit in London, but few people came. Everybody had already seen his paintings, and the Indian Gallery wasn't as exciting without live Indians.

George lived with his daughters in rented rooms at 6 Waterloo Place, making copies of his paintings and publishing another book. *Catlin's Notes of Eight Years' Travels and Residence in Europe* made a little money, but reviews were poor. George was no longer the talk of the town. He was forced to borrow more and more money. He took a job in London, hawking Texas real estate. In his sales pitch, he would hint that gold might be found there, even though he knew it wasn't true. He began to lose his hearing.

George still believed that the U.S. Congress would buy his collection. In 1848 a Congressional committee recommended purchasing the Gallery for $50,000 (about $1 million in today's money), but Congress adjourned before a vote could be taken on the measure. In 1849 an amendment to buy the Gallery was defeated in the Senate by only two votes.

By 1852 George had hit bottom. He had sold some paintings for ten dollars apiece, but it wasn't enough. He couldn't feed and clothe his daughters anymore. The creditors to whom he owed money demanded to be repaid. George's possessions were to be seized and auctioned off to the highest bidder. George was headed for jail.

Filled with "sorrow and shame," George wrote a letter from debtors' prison to Daniel Webster, a former U.S. senator and the current secretary of state. Webster had championed George's earlier appeals to Congress. Now George pleaded with him to save the Indian Gallery.

Henry Clay, Daniel Webster, and John C. Calhoun, three of the giants of the nineteenth-century American political scene, are among the senators shown in this picture. Webster (seated, with his hand to his face, to the left of Clay, who is addressing the Senate) supported George's efforts to sell the Indian Gallery to the government but could not convince enough of his colleagues to vote for the idea.
THE UNITED STATES SENATE, A.D. 1850. ENGRAVING BY R. WHITECHURCH AFTER AN ORIGINAL DRAWING BY P. F. ROTHERMEL, CA. 1855. LIBRARY OF CONGRESS.

After Joseph Harrison, Jr. (1810–74) took possession of the Indian Gallery in 1852, it lay in the basement of a warehouse at the Harrison Boiler Works for more than twenty years.

JOSEPH HARRISON, JR., BY THOMAS BUCHANAN READ. OIL, 1860. COURTESY OF THE PENNSYLVANIA ACADEMY OF THE FINE ARTS, PHILADELPHIA. GIFT OF LELAND HARRISON.

Three weeks later he wrote to Webster again, saying a friend had been able to get him out of jail. But his urgent appeal to Washington failed.

In desperation George sent an ad to the London *Times*: "Catlin's splendid American Indian Collection just about to leave London for all parts of the world. Call and take the last possible look at it before it leaves, and decide upon the pretty and curious things you must covet before it is too late."

No one called.

In the meantime, George had written to Clara's brother, Dudley Gregory, begging him to come and take the girls back to the United States. Dudley arrived a few weeks later, and George had to say goodbye to Libby, Conny, and Louise. The girls, ages fourteen, twelve, and eleven, went to New Jersey to live with the Gregory family.

Officials seized the Indian Gallery. Auctioneers prepared the Gallery for sale. Not only George's paintings but also the precious buffalo robes, medicine bags, peace pipes, and everything else he had collected in his years among the Indians would be sold to pay his debts. All his efforts to honor the "vanishing Indians" would disappear. It was as if a part of his life would be erased.

At the last minute a wealthy American art collector named Joseph Harrison, Jr., offered to pay off George's creditors in return for possession of the Indian Gallery. Harrison owned the largest locomotive-building factory in the world, the Harrison Boiler Works in Philadelphia. He happened to be passing through London on his way home after building a railroad for the czar of Russia. Harrison paid most of George's debts and shipped the Indian Gallery to the United States, where it was tucked away in the basement of a warehouse.

George saw Harrison as a savior. By keeping the Gallery intact and preventing it from being sold off piece by piece, Harrison had saved George's life's work. No one could view the collection in the Philadelphia warehouse, but at least it was back in the United States. If George could raise the money, he could repay Harrison and regain possession.

Not all of Joseph Harrison's motives were noble. He didn't secure the Gallery as a favor to George or because he liked him. Harrison was a shrewd businessman and thought the Gallery was a good investment. It would not be so easy for George to buy it back.

Also, Harrison hadn't paid all of George's debts. There were still others to whom George owed money.

In secret, George fled to Paris. He was fifty-seven years old, penniless, and going deaf. He had lost his family, his Gallery, and his possessions. All he had to his name were the clothes on his back and some drawings and sketches he had managed to sneak out of London.

But he also had the memories of his glorious days in the wilderness among the Indians, and a spirit that would not die.

DREAMING OF GOLD

That summer there was yet another proposal in Congress to buy the Indian Gallery. But though the war with Mexico had ended and some in Congress were aware of George's dire financial situation, again no action was taken. Some said the government had no business spending money on art. Others were distracted by the upcoming election. Fierce debates about slavery and states' rights took center stage.

Meanwhile, George was living by himself in a cheap room in a Paris hotel. He busied himself making copies of his Indian portraits. When he went about, no one recognized him in his shabby clothes. By wintertime he had taken to visiting the national library every day. There he could read and keep warm.

Alexander von Humboldt (1769–1859) spent five years in South America and the next twenty-one years writing about his discoveries. His interests in geology, meteorology, biology, and physics led him to investigate an amazing array of subjects, including magnetic fields, volcanoes, and electric eels.

BARON ALEXANDER VON HUMBOLDT, HALF-LENGTH PORTRAIT, FACING FRONT. PHOTOGRAPHER UNKNOWN, 1850–59. LIBRARY OF CONGRESS.

One of the books George read at the library was a book about traveling in South America. It was written by Alexander von Humboldt, the famous scientist and explorer he had befriended during his happier days in Paris back in 1845. George was fascinated by von Humboldt's story. He began to read every book he could find about South America and to study maps of the continent. When a fellow reader told him about an abandoned gold mine in the Crystal Mountains (*Serra Tumucumaque*) of northern Brazil, piles of gold began to glitter in George's imagination. Perhaps he could sail to South America, find the abandoned mine, and strike it rich. And while he was at it, he could paint the South American Indians.

Without telling a soul, not even his family, George packed his pencils, paints, brushes, and sketchbooks. He scraped together enough money, perhaps from the sale of a few drawings, to buy some Bristol board, a kind of hard, white-coated cardboard that wouldn't rot in the humid jungle. Into a bag he tucked a portfolio filled with copies of his North American Indian portraits, his notes from von Humboldt's book, a couple of maps, a pocket compass, a fishing pole, a Colt pistol, and a six-shot Colt rifle, which he nicknamed "Sam."

Then he got himself a fake passport under an assumed name—to escape the creditors who were still after him—and sailed for Venezuela.

PART FOUR

Wanderings, 1854–61

IN SEARCH OF UNTOLD RICHES

"With no other means on earth than my hands and my brush, and less than half of a life, at best, before me . . . my thoughts . . . tended towards Dame Fortune," George wrote. ". . . Into one of the eccentric adventures of my chequered life I was easily led. . . . Nuggets of gold of all sizes appeared in my dreams."

After a stop in Havana, Cuba, the ship arrived in Venezuela. George felt hopeful. Here was a whole continent to explore, filled with amazing natural wonders, new Indian tribes to paint, and gold to make him rich.

From his writings, it is hard to know where George went first. It seems he traveled by steamer, canoe, foot, horse, and mule, undaunted by the fact that he spoke little Spanish and no Portuguese or *lingua-geral,* a mix of Portuguese and the Tupinambá (Tupi) Indian language.

In company with a German botanist, he crossed the pampas, or prairies—dotted with palm trees, fragrant with wildflowers, and crawling with rattlesnakes. There he painted a war dance and a *Mach-ee-o-a,* or "handsome dance," performed by three young women from a tribe he called the Goo-á-gives.

In the jungle of the Orinoco, George saw sloths hanging from trees by their toenails and alligators that eyed him for dinner. He kept one hand on "Sam" at all times, his trusty rifle lying "*before* me during the day and *in my arms* during the night."

George's Colt pistol and rifle were gifts from Samuel Colt himself, who had opened a factory in London in 1852 and for whom George had painted twelve pictures that were later used in advertisements. The guns may not have been his only protection while traveling in South America. In a letter he claimed to have bought a chain-mail tunic to wear under his shirt.

"The songs of the day are all joyous and cheering," George wrote, ". . . but . . . the animals of the dark steal upon their sleeping, unprotected prey! The frequent roar we often hear of the hungry jaguar—the doleful howlings of the red monkeys—the hooting of owls—and *every* night, the inquisitive *goat-sucker* . . ."

Though it sounded ominous, George's goatsucker was not some kind of bloodsucking vampire but a nocturnal bird that eats insects.

For a while he traveled with an Englishman named Smyth. Smyth wrote that George demonstrated Sam to one tribe by shooting six bull's-eyes into a target more than sixty yards away. When the little boys of the tribe asked if George also had a "young rifle," or handgun, he pulled out his pistol, said it was "very young," and shot some bullets into a palm tree. Using knives, the boys spent several days digging the bullets out of the tree.

Sometimes George collected rocks for his mineral collection, breaking them with a hammer, wetting them with his tongue to see the colors, and putting them into his pocket. According to Smyth, the boys of one tribe said "'they had seen him every morning making his breakfast on stones, and putting others in his pocket for his dinner!' The Indians gave him the name of the Stone Eater."

Through present-day Guyana, Suriname, French Guiana, and Brazil, George painted his way. In the state of Pará, Brazil, he saw a dozen tribes that were known as "Canoe Indians" because they traveled everywhere by canoe, lived in "nests" in the trees, and seldom set foot on dry land. On the Amazon River he encountered Indians who were not used to outsiders. They would glide alongside his boat in their canoes, but if he tried to talk to them, they would slip away. Sometimes he would paint them from a distance, standing on the deck of his boat while the Portuguese boatman kept their attention by playing his violin.

George later wrote that within a few months he had painted at least thirty tribes, including the Muras, Iquitos, Xingus, Tapuyas, Yahuas,

Although this photograph was taken many years after George's visit to Brazil, the huts look exactly like the ones he painted.

INDIAN HUT IN CLEARING ON RIVER BANK, BRAZIL. PHOTOGRAPHER UNKNOWN, CA. 1890–1923. LIBRARY OF CONGRESS.

Mayorunas, and Cocomas. These were not portraits of individual chiefs like the ones he had painted in the 1830s, but more generic, less detailed pictures. The South American Indians were proving somewhat reluctant to be painted, and George had difficulty communicating with them because of his poor hearing. The landscape presented no such problems, however, and he made many sketches of the jungle. Later he wrote that "no pen or pencil can describe the gorgeousness and richness of the overhanging and reflected forests that changed every moment as we passed."

In this painting, three Indians in a canoe are dwarfed by the luxuriant rain forest, where constant heat and moisture help plants grow to enormous sizes.

Entrance to a Lagoon, Shore of the Amazon, by George Catlin. Oil, 1853–54. Image © Board of Trustees, National Gallery of Art, Washington, D.C. Paul Mellon Collection.

All the while, he was dreaming of riches and working his way toward the lost gold mine of the Crystal Mountains. In Belém, on the Amazon, he hired Caesar Bolla, a strapping six-foot-two escaped black Cuban slave. With a couple of traveling companions, a Spanish translator, and some Indian guides, George and Caesar set out to find the mine. Their supplies included the staples of every gold prospector: a sledgehammer for smashing rocks and a tin pan for washing out the gold nuggets.

By boat and then by foot they made their way,

> *wading . . . creeping and crawling, through the vast and sunless [jungle]. . . . Each one carrying his load upon his back as he squeezed and crept through the mazy network of shrubbery and twisted vines. Our Indian guides professed to be "following a road"; but what a road! A road here is where the Indians have . . . cut away the vines and made an opening large enough for a man's body, as he stoops, to pass through.*

The tropical jungle was a new landscape for George, completely different from the eastern woodlands of his childhood, the Great Plains, or the crowded cities of Europe.

"In the fresh air and sunshine at the tops of the trees, which we can never see, there is a busy and chattering neighbourhood of parrots and monkeys," he wrote, "but all below is a dark and silent matted solitude, in which a falling leaf, from want of wind, may be a month in reaching the ground, and where a man may be tracked by the broken cobwebs he leaves behind him."

As they walked, nuts and nutshells would fall onto their heads, dropped by monkeys and birds from tree limbs far above. At night, they swatted at mosquitoes while howler monkeys sang to them. George's legs were covered with so many red ticks that he had to scrape the insects off with a knife.

The white men and Caesar Bolla carried rifles, while the Indian guides were armed with blowguns and poisoned arrows. Both types of weapons came in handy, especially when the group encountered a herd of peccaries, a kind of wild pig with razor-sharp teeth. Bok-ar, one of the guides, killed the largest peccary with a single poisoned arrow, shot from his blowgun. The herd then fell upon the dead animal, tearing it to pieces. Caesar fired his rifle into the air, and the animals disappeared into the jungle.

On the far side of the jungle, George and his traveling companions reached a prairie, where they visited the village of a tribe he called the Zurumati. There they traded some supplies for a mule. As they continued on, the land grew more hilly and rugged, until they found themselves clambering over rocky hills and through deserted ravines.

George wrote that Smyth was often treed by peccaries. Here, George and a Caribbe Indian come to his rescue. *A Fight with Peccaries—Caribbe,* by George Catlin. Oil, 1854/1869. Image © Board of Trustees, National Gallery of Art, Washington, D.C. Paul Mellon Collection.

Finally, they reached the Crystal Mountains. They searched the streams for traces of gold by swishing water and pebbles in the tin pan, but they found nothing. Then the mule stepped on the pan and broke through the bottom. That was the end of panning for gold.

Maybe they could find a vein of gold running through the rock cliffs. They followed a river until they came to a gorge filled with huge boulders of grayish rose quartz that had fallen from the cliff above. Each one weighed several hundred tons. In one of the boulders George spied a cluster of shiny nuggets, the largest of which was the size of a pea. He and his companions attacked the cluster with chisels and a screwdriver, their hearts racing. With everyone's hopes high, Caesar began to pound at the rock with the sledgehammer. As his arms descended for one more mighty blow, the hammerhead separated from its handle and fell into the river. Frantically, they searched for it, but the stream was deep and they kept slipping and sliding in the rushing water. The hammerhead was lost.

With no tin pan and no sledgehammer, there was little chance of finding more than a few nuggets here and there in the gravel at the edge of the stream. For two or three days they wandered from ravine to ravine, desperately hoping to find an ancient path or some Indians who could point them in a more promising direction.

Food and supplies were running low. Gradually, the truth began to sink in: there would be no great riches, no gleaming mountain of gold. Painfully disappointed, George and his companions gave up their search and trudged back to the Amazon Valley. The entire expedition had yielded only two ounces of gold.

But, George later wrote, he was not crushed by defeat. He hadn't found the legendary lost mine of the Crystal Mountains, but in his first few months in South America he had discovered something more precious than gold—his taste for adventure had come roaring back to life. Filled with a new enthusiasm, he set out with Caesar to explore the rest

The Omáguan language was once spoken by more than a million people in western Brazil and northeastern Peru. Today fewer than a dozen people speak Omáguan.

THREE OMAGUA MEN, BY GEORGE CATLIN. OIL, 1854/1869. IMAGE © BOARD OF TRUSTEES, NATIONAL GALLERY OF ART, WASHINGTON, D.C. PAUL MELLON COLLECTION.

of South America and paint its Indians. Their journey would eventually take them to two other continents as well.

George and Caesar rode across the Pampa del Sacramento and voyaged up the Ucayali by canoe. There George painted Indians from several tribes, including Omáguas, Conibos, and Shipibos. Like many of the Great Plains Indians, these South American Indians had never seen portrait paintings before. Some were frightened by George's work. One Conibo medicine man was disturbed, as the Lakota Sioux had been years before, because the eyes in George's paintings stayed open all night. He thought George wanted to steal the Indians' skins and put them in a museum. The Conibos became so upset that the only way George could preserve his pictures was to paint over them with clay. When he left the village, he washed the clay off.

Following a sometimes perilous route, George and Caesar crossed the Andes Mountains, the highest range in South America. In Lima, Peru, on the Pacific coast, they boarded a ship bound for San Francisco. There were tribes on the west coast of North America that George had never painted. And he had long ago vowed to paint them all.

NORTHWARD ON THE *SALLY ANNE*

Aboard the *Sally Anne* George touched up his sketches and organized his supplies. When the ship arrived in San Francisco, George and Caesar didn't stay long. They found the booming gold-rush town much too civilized. Instead, they reboarded the *Sally Anne* and headed farther north.

Soon the snowcapped mountains of the Pacific Northwest gleamed in the distance. The ship put into port in Astoria, Oregon Territory, where the crew traded beads, blankets, and knives for dried salmon, whale blubber, and oysters. Continuing up the coast, they stopped on Vancouver Island, in Canada. There George admired the way the Tla-o-qui-ahts, the Toquahts, and other Nuu-chah-nulth Indian groups made dugout canoes using mussel-shell tools, stone hammers, and chisels tipped with elk horn.

As many as a hundred men and women might work to create and decorate a dugout canoe as large as the one in this picture.
LAUNCHING A CANOE—NAYAS INDIANS, BY GEORGE CATLIN. OIL, 1855/1869. IMAGE © BOARD OF TRUSTEES, NATIONAL GALLERY OF ART, WASHINGTON, D.C. PAUL MELLON COLLECTION.

In a Tla-o-qui-aht village George sketched a chief, his wife, and their child. As he was working, someone yelled, "Whale ashore!" The entire village jumped into their canoes and sped off down the coast. George returned to the *Sally Anne,* and the next day he watched from the deck as hundreds of Indians ate, drank, sang, and danced around a giant sperm whale that had been beached by a storm.

Northward the *Sally Anne* sailed, according to George, past the Queen Charlotte Islands and into Russian territory—present-day Alaska and the Aleutian Islands—and across the Bering Strait into Siberia. Here, in the farthest reaches of northeastern Asia, George wrote that he sketched the Koriaks of the Kamchatka Peninsula, who lived in houses made of earth, with a door in the top.

Then, George said, the ship turned around and headed back to North America, where he recounted painting people he called Athabascas and Esquimaux (probably Inuit or Yupik) in present-day Alaska; the Salish, who lived in present-day British Columbia; and the Haidas of the Queen Charlotte Islands, who sported blocks of wood in

This photograph, taken more than forty years after George visited the Arctic region, shows an Inuit house of the type George would have seen. The Inuit had to be skilled hunters and fishermen to survive in the harsh climate. On top of the hut are sealskin floats, attached to harpoons.
INUIT HUT AND FAMILY, BY EDWARD S. CURTIS. PHOTOGRAPH, CA. 1899. LIBRARY OF CONGRESS.

their lower lips and wore capes woven of mountain-sheep wool and wild-dog hair. The Haida chief's daughter, George wrote, had a cape "wonderfully knitted with spun-yarn of beautiful colours . . . and bordered with a fringe of eighteen inches in length, the work of three women for one year, I was told, and its price, five horses. . .

"Vanity is the same all the world over," he added. ". . . Rings in the nose or rings in the ears, they are all the same."

Whether the chief's daughter reminded George of his own daughters in faraway New Jersey he did not say. If they had any idea of his whereabouts during the 1850s, it was vague at best. No letters to them from this period have survived.

Back in the Oregon Territory, George and Caesar left the *Sally Anne* and sailed up the Columbia River, which forms the border between present-day Oregon and Washington. With a horse, two mules, and an Indian guide they trekked east toward the Rocky Mountains, stopping for George to paint the Clatsops, Chinooks, Klickitats, Walla Wallas, Nez Perces, and Spokanes. Then they made their way through the valleys of the Snake and Salmon rivers into present-day Idaho, where they came upon a Crow village.

There George felt as if he were with old friends. When he opened his portfolio to show some paintings, he recalled, "one of the party gave a sudden piercing yelp, and sprang upon his feet and commenced dancing in the most violent jumps and starts . . . 'Bi-éets-e-cure! Bi-éets-e-cure!'" the young man shouted.

He had recognized a portrait of Bi-éets-e-cure, The Very Sweet Man, whom George had painted at Fort Union in 1832. A few of the men ran out, returning shortly with Bi-éets-e-cure.

"I instantly recognized him," George wrote, "and rising up, he took about half a minute to look me full in the eyes, without moving a muscle or winking, when he exclaimed, 'how! how!' (yes, yes), and shook me heartily by the hand."

As George continued to show his pictures, the Crows recognized a painting of a chief who had died. When George told them that more than one hundred thousand white people had seen the chief's face, all the men rose and embraced him.

Soon it was time to return to the Pacific coast. George and Caesar took a different route back so that George could study the geology of the mountains. It was hard going. Their Indian guide had returned to his village, and the terrain was rocky and dry. In this desolate landscape there was hardly any grass for the horse and mules. They had to lead the animals most of the way rather than ride them, because the path was so steep. After five days they ran out of food for themselves.

Luckily, a few hours later they encountered a wagon train bound for the Oregon Territory. The emigrants, as these travelers were called, offered to share their boiled pork and beans and their hard biscuits. For two days George and Caesar rode with the wagon train, but it was so slow that they soon left it behind. A week's trek brought them eventually to Fort Walla Walla, in present-day Washington. From there they continued westward to the Columbia River.

Back in Portland, Oregon Territory, George and Caesar boarded a ship bound for San Diego, in southern California. George had never painted members of the Apache tribe of the Southwest, whom he considered "the most powerful and most hostile tribe in America." It was now or never.

THE RESTLESS TRAVELER

In San Diego, George bought horses, and he and Caesar rode east. Following the Gila River across present-day Arizona and New Mexico, they eventually turned north through the mountains toward Santa Fe. For hundreds and hundreds of miles, all the land through which they passed was Apache hunting territory.

After several weeks they finally encountered some Apaches, and

The covered-wagon train in this picture is similar to the one George and Caesar encountered.
EMIGRANT PARTY ON THE ROAD TO CALIFORNIA. HAND-COLORED ENGRAVING, 1850. LIBRARY OF CONGRESS.

despite the tribe's reputation, George was able to make friends with them. They were impressed by his honest manner and could see that George and Caesar were travelers, not soldiers, and posed no threat.

George and Caesar were invited to stay in an Apache village, and George was allowed to paint. The Apaches, like the Comanches, prided themselves on their horsemanship and on their skill with bows and arrows. George sketched an Apache shooting competition in which the mounted men, in war dress and war paint, galloped their horses at full speed in a huge circle, shooting at targets cut into the ground.

The rapidity with which their arrows are placed upon the string and sent is a mystery to the bystander, and must be seen to be believed. No repeating arms ever yet constructed are so rapid, nor any arm, at that little distance, more fatal. Each arrow, as it flies, goes with a yelp, and each bow is bent with a "wuhgh!" which seems to strain its utmost sinew, and every muscle of the archer.

At the end of the competition, prizes were awarded, and George and Caesar were treated to a feast.

Speed and accuracy were put to the test during Apache archery competitions.

ARCHERY OF THE APACHEES [SIC], BY GEORGE CATLIN. OIL ON PAPER MOUNTED ON PAPERBOARD, CA. 1855. AMON CARTER MUSEUM, FORT WORTH, TEXAS. 1986.40.

On the road again, George and Caesar came upon some Apache women, children, and elderly men whose village had been destroyed by United States soldiers. All the younger men of the village had been killed. It was the first sign for George and Caesar of a war between the Apaches and the United States. George realized it would be foolish to continue through Apache territory, and he and Caesar turned southeast toward the Rio Grande.

The dry desert landscape could not have been more different from the steamy jungles and Arctic wastelands they had passed through the year before. But whatever the setting, danger lurked.

One night, as Caesar was tending the fire, two grizzly bears came upon their campsite. Caesar took a burning piece of wood and hurled it at one of the them.

"The firebrand fell a few feet before it, when the beast sprang upon it with both paws, and seized it in its mouth!" George wrote. "He dropped it, and wheeling about, and crying in the most piteous manner, retreated, wiping his nose and his paws upon the grass." The other bear picked up the burning branch and just as quickly dropped it. The bears ran off, and George and Caesar built two big fires and took turns keeping watch all night.

A few days later they came upon a cabin, where a settler fed them steak, pan-baked bread, and coffee sweetened with molasses. When George praised the delicious steak, the woman said of course it was delicious—it was panther meat!

Finally, they reached the Rio Grande, and George sold the horses and bought a canoe. He and Caesar paddled downstream eight hundred

Adult male grizzlies can weigh 1,200 pounds and stand eight feet tall on their hind legs. George painted one with a mouse so that people who had never seen a grizzly could understand how large it was.
PORTRAITS OF A GRIZZLY BEAR AND MOUSE, LIFE SIZE, BY GEORGE CATLIN. OIL, 1846–48. SMITHSONIAN AMERICAN ART MUSEUM. GIFT OF MRS. JOSEPH HARRISON, JR.

miles to Matamoros, near the Gulf of Mexico. From there they sailed to the port town of Sisal on the Yucatán Peninsula. After painting some native Mayas and trekking into the jungle to visit the ancient ruined city of Uxmal, George sailed back to Europe.

Caesar stayed behind. He had met his true love—a woman who sold oranges on a dock—and he was settling down.

George was now nearly sixty, but his travels were not yet done. In Prussia he met with his old friend Alexander von Humboldt, who convinced him that there was more exploring to do in South America. And who better to do it than George?

"If I were a younger man I would join you in the expedition at once!" von Humboldt wrote in a farewell letter to George in September 1855. ". . . Let nothing stop you—you are on a noble mission, and the Great Spirit will protect you."

With money from the sale of some paintings to the king and queen of Prussia, George returned to South America. He wanted to paint more Indians, of course, but he was also interested in studying ocean currents and geology. Both he and von Humboldt thought that the study of nature could help them answer questions about how and why people settled in different parts of the world. At the time, some scientists thought that the first human beings had originated in the Middle East and then spread to other continents. Others thought that the native peoples of North and South America had developed independently. If it could be shown that ocean currents flowed in certain directions, this would be evidence that ancient Indians had migrated across the ocean from a common place. It would support the theory that all races shared a common ancestry.

Scientists were also interested in tracing the connections between diverse languages for clues as to how one group of people might be related to another. The study of animals, plants, weather, and soil could also yield information about the history of human settlement and the development of cultures.

MAP TK

The debate had implications for the treatment of Indians, as well as for the institution of slavery. It would be harder to justify slavery or regard Indians as "savages" if Europeans, native peoples of North and South America, and Africans were all related.

George's plan was to collect fossils and rocks, measure rock formations, observe the flow of streams, and note the dimensions of caves. Meanwhile, he would compare Indian legends and languages and paint as many additional tribes as he could. If he had some rip-roaring adventures while he was at it, so much the better.

During these years of travel and exploration, George made money where and when he could. Sometimes he sold drawings or painted portraits on commission, though now that photography had been invented, portraits were not as popular as they had previously been. At one point he sold some land in which he had invested and was lucky enough to earn almost $1,500—more than $30,000 in today's money. Still wary of his English creditors, he continued to use a fake passport through the 1850s and rarely communicated with friends and family in the United States. In a way, these were George's "lost years." He was certainly lost to his daughters, who continued to be supported by the Gregorys.

And so, swept away on the tide of his own enthusiasm, George crossed the Atlantic once again. Through the West Indies and along the eastern coast of South America; south to Rio de Janeiro and Buenos Aires; up the Paraná River and down the Uruguay River; past Patagonia to the Strait of Magellan and into Tierra del Fuego at the southern tip of the continent; north along the coast to Valparaiso, Chile; onward to the volcanoes of Cotopaxi and Chimborazo in Ecuador; then northward to Colombia and Panama—George journeyed for two more years.

He measured ocean currents off the islands of Jamaica, St. Thomas, Antigua, Grenada, Trinidad, and Tortuga. He painted Payágua Indians in Paraguay—a tribe who dined mainly on fish and turtles and who

were even taller than the Osages and the Cheyennes—and the Botocudos of Brazil, who wore blocks of wood in their lips like the Haidas of the Pacific Northwest. In Corrientes, Argentina, he hired a man named José Alzar as an assistant, guide, and translator. Together they canoed the Paraguay and the Uruguay, shooting jaguars and eating their tails wrapped in wild cabbage leaves and roasted under the embers of a campfire. "Nothing that ever was cooked exceeds it in deliciousness of flavour, and pleasure of digestion," George declared.

These journeys were often dangerous, and George had some close calls. One day he shot at a jaguar and missed. The animal attacked, and George fell backward thirty feet down a riverbank and was knocked unconscious. José dragged him into the canoe and quickly pushed off into the current. As George came to, his arm began to hurt. The jaguar's teeth had left puncture wounds between his elbow and wrist, from which blood was flowing. His shirt had been ripped by the animal's claws, and two furrows ran down his back. Luckily, the wounds were not deep. Soon George was painting Indians again.

The American artist Frederic Church, like George, was inspired by Alexander von Humboldt to visit South America in the 1850s. But instead of painting Indians, Church produced dramatic landscapes.
COTOPAXI, BY FREDERIC CHURCH. OIL, 1855. SMITHSONIAN AMERICAN ART MUSEUM

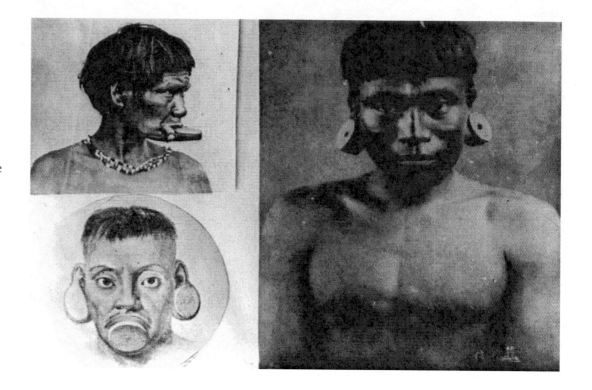

The word *botocudos* comes from the Portuguese *botoque*, or "plug." Several Brazilian tribes were called Botocudos because of the wooden plugs they wore in their pierced ears and lower lips. The practice had largely disappeared by the twentieth century.

BRAZIL. 3 BOTOCUDOS INDIAN MEN WITH LARGE EAR AND MOUTH RINGS, BY FRANK G. CARPENTER. TWO PHOTOGRAPHS AND A REPRODUCTION OF A DRAWING, CREATED BETWEEN 1890 AND 1923. LIBRARY OF CONGRESS.

Later, George rode south into the pampas of Argentina with José and some new friends who were part Portuguese and part Auca Indian. Among the Aucas (now known as the Mapuches) George learned how to catch wild horses with a bola, a rawhide cord that was used like a lasso. Together they hunted guanacos (a kind of llama) and went on an "ostrich chase," during which the Mapuches, mounted on horses, drove *nandu* birds out of vast thistle patches and then caught them with bolas.

George, José, and the Mapuches also hunted flamingos at a place George called the Grand Saline, a salt lake in central Argentina. It was summer, and the lake had turned to mud. Swarms of fireflies were so thick that the light from their bodies "almost extinguished the darkness of night," he wrote.

Millions of white flamingos had built nests on the salt flats. George and one of the Indians decided to take a closer look. Tucking branches into their belts until they were covered with leaves from head to toe, they crept forward through the mud and came within a hundred feet of some of the nests. Female birds were sitting on eggs while males stood next to them on one leg, fast asleep. Other birds were plucking worms from the mud.

One of the tallest birds became curious. He came right up to George with a mouth full of worms. George burst into laughter. The bird screamed, and George fired his rifle. Thousands of birds rose into the air. "Those that were near were wheeling about in the air, like a cloud above us, and shadowing the earth around us; and as the alarm was general, those rising more slowly in the extreme distance looked like a white fog streaming up from the ground," he wrote.

George shot at one of the birds, and it fell. The flock flew down and around George, beating their wings in his face, then took off. He shot several more birds, and the Indians collected the wings. The feathers would fetch a good price in the city.

In later years George remembered these South American adventures as happy ones. He liked nothing better than living by his wits, hunting for his dinner, meeting and painting new tribes. If he missed his family in the United States, he didn't say.

George could have settled down somewhere in South America and lived the rest of his life there. But something kept him on the move—restlessness, love of adventure, an obsession with painting Indians. Maybe, too, he was running away from the shame of bankruptcy, the humiliation of being unable to provide for his daughters, and the sorrow of losing his wife and son.

And then, in the late 1850s, George turned up again in Europe. Exactly when he returned is hard to say; in his books and letters he was vague about dates. It is almost impossible to trace his routes with certainty, and some of his adventures may even have taken place on a third trip to South America in 1858–60. But evidently, by 1860 enough time had passed that his English creditors had no claim on him anymore.

By then he was living in Brussels, Belgium, surviving on money from

sales of a book he had written for children, *Life Amongst the Indians.* He also published *The Breath of Life, or Mal-respiration,* in which he claimed that Indians enjoyed better health than whites because they slept on their backs, with their mouths closed. During the 1860s he was in touch with his family, but he didn't go to see his daughters or invite them to visit him. He must have felt they were better off with their wealthy uncle in the United States. Meanwhile, he wrote and painted. But his traveling days were over.

PART FIVE

Home at Last, 1861–72

~~~~~~~~~

WITH PEN AND PAINTBRUSH

In April 1861 George wrote to his youngest daughter, Louise, who was then almost twenty. The letter started with an apology.

> *My dear, Sweet little Louise,*
>
> *You can imagine some what of the shame, the pain, the anguish of an affectionate and loving parent so long separated from those he most loves . . . but you can never know the whole of it. . . . I have seen much and I have done much & I have traveled much. . . .*

He proceeded to tell Louise all the places he had visited since they had last seen each other: Siberia, the Rocky Mountains, the Amazon, Venezuela, Bolivia, Peru, Ecuador—the list went on. It was as if he was trying to impress her by naming so many places and explaining how hard he had been working.

I have had nothing but my own hands, with the talent which
the Almighty gave me . . . to pay my way. . . . If my life had
been thrown away in idleness or dissipations during these
long years of absence there would be no excuse for me,
I would be a monster, and I should have no right to ask
forgiveness of my dear little angels, but I have been constantly
at work, and still am so.

George was asking for forgiveness and telling Louise how painful it had been for him to be separated from his children for so long. And yet the tone of his letter, the first to any of his daughters in nine years, was strangely disconnected. He didn't seem to understand how *they* must have felt or how much they must have missed him.

But selfish or not, for George work came first. In a little studio in Brussels, with a cage full of white mice for company, he worked on hundreds of new Indian paintings and drawings. He sketched these from memory or made copies from the small number of paintings he had saved from his creditors, from old sketches of work in the original Indian Gallery, or from illustrations in the books he had written years earlier. He called these new paintings "cartoons" and was determined to create an entire collection of them, the Cartoon Collection. He had lost the original Indian Gallery; he would paint himself another one.

George did not use the word "cartoon" in the way it is understood today. To him, "cartoon" referred to his method of creating new work based on rough outlines or tracings of old paintings. Eventually, these copies of early works made up about half of the new collection. The rest consisted of the paintings on Bristol board that he had created while traveling in the 1850s.

Every day after painting, George went to the same café, where he would dine by himself on steak and potatoes and write for a while. There were days when he hardly spoke to anyone. By now he was com-

This photograph shows some of the ornate buildings of La Grande Place, the central market square of Brussels, at the end of the nineteenth century. It looks much the same today.

LA GRANDE PLACE, BRUSSELS, BELGIUM. PHOTOGRAPHER UNKNOWN. PHOTOMECHANICAL PRINT, CA. 1890–1900. LIBRARY OF CONGRESS.

pletely deaf and walked with a cane because of a bad knee. Otherwise, he was in good health and just as determined as ever.

General A. L. Chetlain, the U.S. consul in Brussels, often visited him. Chetlain recalled that George was

> quite robust and active for one of his advanced years. He was a charming talker, but his hearing was so impaired it was with great difficulty one could talk to him. . . . He seemed to have few acquaintances even among his brother artists. . . . He talked to me often about his collection . . . and expressed a hope . . . that all his works might be brought together and placed in the hands of the Government of the United States. . . . He evidently felt [great] anxiety for the future of his life

Henry Rowe Schoolcraft was a Washington insider who was able to get government funding for his projects.

HENRY ROWE SCHOOLCRAFT. ENGRAVING, 1857. FROM SCHOOLCRAFT, HISTORY OF THE INDIAN TRIBES OF THE UNITED STATES. . . . PHILADELPHIA: J. B. LIPPINCOTT & CO., 1857, VOL. 6.

long work . . . and always took pride in calling himself the "friend of the Indian." . . . He never alluded to his family or family affairs, and gave no reason for the singular life he chose to live in Brussels.

George's solitary life was due, in part, to his deafness. He was also busily at work. During these years he wrote three more books, including *Last Rambles Amongst the Indians of the Rocky Mountains and the Andes* (1867) and *The Lifted and Subsided Rocks of America* (1870). But the book that meant the most to him was *O-kee-pa: A Religious Ceremony, and Other Customs of the Mandans,* published in 1867.

The Mandan tribe of the Missouri River Valley had been almost completely wiped out by smallpox in 1837, five years after George had visited them. Even after all this time, he felt the loss keenly. He had never forgotten his friend Máh-to-tóh-pa, Four Bears, or the brave young men who had undergone the trials of the *O-kee-pa* ritual. He thought it was his duty to help the world remember the Mandans.

George had another reason for publishing *O-kee-pa.* A man named Henry Rowe Schoolcraft had written an enormous six-volume book about the North American Indians in which he had claimed that there was no such thing as the *O-kee-pa* ceremony. He had accused George of imagining the whole thing. Worse yet, Schoolcraft's book was an official publication of the United States government, and thousands of copies had been shipped off as gifts to governments and libraries around the world. Schoolcraft, who had lived in Washington, D.C., had also been influential in the long-ago Congressional debates about buying the Indian Gallery. George believed that Schoolcraft had persuaded people to vote against the purchase, and had never forgiven him.

Schoolcraft died in 1864, but his book lived on. George was furious. It was as if Schoolcraft had called him a liar. And so George wrote *O-kee-pa* to make sure the whole world knew the truth.

But it was too late. Because Schoolcraft's book was sponsored by the government, people believed it, and George's *O-kee-pa* didn't sell many copies. George wrote letters of protest to the U.S. government. He even thought of going to Washington, D.C., then changed his mind because his deafness made it so hard for him to talk with people. After devoting his whole life to painting and writing about the Indians, he was angry that his honesty and integrity had been attacked.

George desperately wanted to save his reputation. He had been hoping that the United States or some other government would buy his new paintings, the Cartoon Collection. And he cherished a dream that he could get back his original collection, the old Indian Gallery, which still lay in crates in the basement of Joseph Harrison's warehouse in Philadelphia. If only he could convince Congress to buy it! His long-treasured dream still haunted him.

In 1868 George asked his youngest brother, Francis, to visit him in Brussels. He wanted to show Francis his new paintings and hoped that Francis would help him to arrange an exhibit in Washington. The brothers hadn't seen each other in twenty-nine years, but Francis agreed to come.

Francis kept a diary during his visit. George, he wrote, "is full of his anecdotes and fun making the whole time—Works from early light till dark every day." Of George's painting habits, he wrote: "He must work as long as he has life—can't be idle a

George at the age of seventy-two, photographed in Brussels, Belgium. *GEORGE CATLIN, 1868.* PHOTOGRAPHER UNKNOWN. IMAGE COURTESY OF GEORGE CATLIN PAPERS, 1821–1904 & 1946, IN THE ARCHIVES OF AMERICAN ART, SMITHSONIAN INSTITUTION.

moment. Some dark stormy days—too dark to see his work—then he is unhappy."

George told Francis that he wouldn't leave Brussels "until he finishes his work and gives the world a chance to see what he has done for the noblest race (he says) that ever trod the earth. If the Indian has a friend, it is *G. Catlin*."

George imagined a triumphant return to Washington, where he would once again be the talk of the town. Before bringing his new paintings to the United States, he planned to exhibit them in Italy, Prussia, Persia, and Russia.

Francis returned to the United States and tried to arrange an exhibit in Washington, but no one was interested in George Catlin or his work. The country was still recovering from the Civil War. Out west the U.S. Army was fighting brutal battles with Indian tribes. And America's taste in art had changed. Now people wanted grand landscape paintings, such as those of Frederic Church, Albert Bierstadt, and Thomas Moran, which inspired in them a sense of national pride.

This illustration from *Harper's Weekly* magazine shows a battle between the U.S. Army and Cheyenne Indians that took place in what is now Beecher Island, Colorado.

Engagement of Colonel Forsyth's Command with the Indians at Small Island, September 17, 1868. Wood engraving, 1868. Library of Congress.

Another of the Catlin brothers, Richard, wrote to Francis: "I don't know anything about the value of [George's] works, but know there is no love for Indians in this country in these times."

Francis wrote to George that he wasn't having much success. But George was not discouraged. He simply refused to believe what he was being told.

By the summer of 1870 the paintings were ready. George exhibited them in Brussels, then decided to skip the rest of his grand tour of Europe and central Asia and take the paintings directly to New York City. The New-York Historical Society had written to inquire about the original Indian Gallery.

George was thrilled—perhaps too thrilled. He named a price so

Americans felt that images of the landscape were morally uplifting because the landscape was sacred, created by God to inspire awe in human beings. In 1872 Thomas Moran sold this gigantic (7' x 12') painting to Congress. It shows two tiny figures dwarfed by a vast wilderness.

THE GRAND CANYON OF THE YELLOWSTONE, BY THOMAS MORAN. OIL, 1872. THE U.S. DEPARTMENT OF THE INTERIOR MUSEUM, WASHINGTON, D.C.

When George returned to the United States, he posed for a photograph dressed in rustic clothes and a flamboyant fur hat, surrounded by Indian blankets. Perhaps he thought this image of him as an authentic man of the western frontier would help to sell his work.

GEORGE CATLIN, BY R. STANLEY FREEMAN. PHOTOGRAPH, 1870. VIRGINIA MUSEUM OF FINE ARTS, RICHMOND. THE PAUL MELLON COLLECTION. © VIRGINIA MUSEUM OF FINE ARTS.

high—$120,000 for both the original Indian Gallery and the Cartoon Collection (about $1.7 million in today's money)—that the Society never even answered his letter. He wrote to them again a few months later, dropping the price to $50,000 for just the original Gallery. But the Society had lost interest. No matter—he still thought he could convince Congress to buy the new paintings.

At about the same time, an English collector bought one of his albums of drawings. With the proceeds, George said goodbye to Brussels and boarded a ship for the last long journey of his life. After thirty-one years, he was finally going home.

ALONE IN THE TOWER

In the fall of 1870 George was met at the dock in New York City by his three daughters and his brother Francis. He hadn't seen the girls for eighteen years. They had grown up, and the country had, too. A railroad now crossed the Great Plains, reaching all the way to the Pacific Ocean. Millions of acres of forest had been cut down and turned into farmland. Much of the wilderness of his youth was gone.

But nothing could stop George. He printed a catalog, bought an ad in the newspaper, hung six hundred paintings, and opened a show in October at the Sommerville Gallery on Fifth Avenue. Admission: fifty cents (about seven dollars today).

George waited for the crowds. The press showed little interest, and few people came. By November the show had closed. New York had forgotten George Catlin.

It was a great blow. Fortunately, Joseph Henry, the director of the Smithsonian Institution in Washington, D.C., was an old acquaintance from Albany. Although years earlier Joseph had been opposed to exhibiting art in the Smithsonian, he now felt that George's work was an important historical record of Indian cultures. He invited George to show his new paintings in the National Museum, part of the Smithsonian.

The museum was in a red brick building known as "the Castle" because it looked like a medieval palace. In February 1872 George shipped his work to Washington, rented rooms about a mile from the museum, and hung his show. Joseph gave George a room to use as a painting studio in one of the towers of the Castle.

George thought the show would bring him respect and attention. He still believed Congress would be moved to buy his work. In his little room in the tower he painted and wrote letters to Congress.

In my old age, after I have devoted a long life of hard labor and all that I have possessed in the world for the history of our country, I am suffering intensely in feelings from the fear that the six hundred Indian portraits and other paintings . . . may be cast upon the world without the finish and arrangement which they require."

The Smithsonian Institution was established by the U.S. government in 1846 with money donated in the will of British scientist James Smithson. The building shown here, called "the Castle," was completed in 1855 and still stands on the National Mall. Today the Smithsonian's nineteen museums and nine research centers own more than 136 million objects, artworks, and specimens.
SMITHSONIAN INSTITUTE, 1860–65. PHOTOGRAPH, L. C. HANDY STUDIO, BETWEEN 1860 AND 1880. LIBRARY OF CONGRESS.

Joseph Henry (1797–1878) was a physics professor at Princeton University and one of the most renowned scientists in the United States when he was appointed head of the Smithsonian Institution in 1846.

JOSEPH HENRY, PORTRAIT. PHOTOGRAPHER UNKNOWN. DAGUERREOTYPE, CA. 1845–50. COURTESY OF CHICAGO HISTORY MUSEUM; ICHI-10694.

He was willing to sell his work for $65,000. It would be enough to pay for the new paintings and rescue the original Indian Gallery from the warehouse basement in Philadelphia. His life's work could finally belong to the American people.

As Joseph Henry spent time with George that spring, he came to agree. Joseph felt that Congress had wronged George by ignoring him for so long and that Schoolcraft's accusations had been unfair, if not criminal.

But even Joseph's support couldn't win enough votes in Congress. Some politicians still thought George should give his paintings to the museum for nothing. The rest paid no attention.

With a sinking heart, George realized that the only reason his paintings were hanging in the museum was because of his friendship with Joseph Henry. He began to see that Congress was not going to buy anything and that he would never recover his original Indian Gallery.

In the summer of 1872 George became ill. The doctor who examined him realized there was something seriously wrong. George had kidney disease, and his heart was failing. The doctor told Joseph, but he didn't tell George.

Joseph set up a cot in the tower room so that George could sleep there. For a while George was too weak to work. Lying there in the tower, all he could think about was what would become of his paintings.

From time to time over the next two months, George felt a little better and would rouse himself to paint or write. Joseph wrote to Dudley Gregory, George's brother-in-law in New Jersey: "Mr. Catlin, although very ill is not confined to his bed . . . his physician has no hope for his recovery . . . Mr. Catlin is not fully aware of the hopelessness . . . and the Doctor has thought it best to allow him to continue painting as far as his strength will permit."

At the end of October, Joseph told George to prepare a will so that his daughters could inherit his paintings. George understood: He was not going to recover.

Two days later Joseph wrote that George was no longer painting but was "not in an unhappy state of mind." He praised George's work and said he was "esteemed above anyone" as an expert on American Indians.

On a rainy night in early November, George was helped into a carriage and driven to the Gregory home in Jersey City, New Jersey. There his daughters took care of him.

George was dying, but when he could muster the strength, he would walk around the room, saying, "Oh, if I was down in the valley of the Amazon I could walk off this weakness."

To the very end, he couldn't stop worrying about the paintings he had left behind in Washington. Surely Congress couldn't ignore a lifetime of work. Surely the politicians would realize the value of his paintings. Eventually, they would see the importance of what he had done. He never gave up hope that Congress would come through.

But it was not to be. Early in the morning of December 23, 1872, the dying painter asked, "What will become of my Gallery?" A few hours later, he passed away.

George was buried in Brooklyn, New York, next to his wife and son. Meanwhile, the original Indian Gallery lay rotting in the basement of the Harrison Boiler Works in Philadelphia, only a hundred miles from his grave.

THE FATE OF THE INDIAN GALLERY

In 1873, "as an act of justice to the memory of the late Mr. Catlin, and as a verification of the truth of his account of a very interesting ceremony among the Mandan Indians," the annual report of the Smithsonian Institution published an essay and letter supporting

George's version of the *O-kee-pa*. At last the truth was known. Some of the Mandans had indeed survived the smallpox epidemic of 1837. Witnesses reported seeing *O-kee-pa* ceremonies as late as 1869.

In 1874 Joseph Harrison, Jr., died. The crates containing the Indian Gallery were taken out of the warehouse. The buffalo robes and clothing had been eaten by moths and mice, the tipis and feathered headdresses ruined by smoke and water damage from two fires. But miraculously, after twenty years in storage, most of the paintings were still intact. Workers buried the rotted artifacts in the yard and moved the paintings and a few surviving artifacts to drier quarters. There the remnants of the Gallery sat for five years until Harrison's widow, Sarah, agreed to donate them to the Smithsonian.

"There were about 450 paintings and much buckskin and fur," wrote Thomas Donaldson, a lawyer and friend of the Smithsonian's new director, who received the collection. "A vast amount of fur robes and the like had been buried in the yard of the Harrison Boiler Works. . . . The paintings were in ancient black wood frames made by Mr.

The Indian Gallery now hangs in the Smithsonian American Art Museum's Renwick Gallery in Washington, D.C.

The Indian Gallery in the Renwick. Photographer unknown. Smithsonian American Art Museum.

Catlin and in wretched condition. . . . The collection filled an entire freight car."

Donaldson spent the next five years restoring and researching the Indian Gallery. The collection was exhibited at the Smithsonian in 1884, then tucked away for decades in a small room where scholars could visit. In the mid-twentieth century the paintings were cleaned and restored, and many have since been shown in cities all over the United States and Europe. Today their permanent home is the Smithsonian American Art Museum, where they are considered a "crown jewel" of the museum's collection.

The Cartoon Collection that George Catlin created late in his life was inherited by his daughters. In 1912 Libby sold it to the American Museum of Natural History in New York. It was later acquired by collector Paul Mellon, who donated most of it to the National Gallery of Art in Washington, D.C.

And so, because of the unexpected twists and turns of history, visitors to Washington can now view in one day what it took George a lifetime to create. Throughout that long life he had dreamed that his work would someday belong to the American people. Though he died without seeing his dream fulfilled, in the end his wish came true.

After the Spanish introduced horses to North America in the sixteenth century, the animals became indispensable to the Plains Indians. With horses, it was much easier to hunt buffalo.

BUFFALO CHASE OVER PRAIRIE BLUFFS, BY GEORGE CATLIN. OIL, 1832–33. SMITHSONIAN AMERICAN ART MUSEUM. GIFT OF MRS. JOSEPH HARRISON, JR.

Afterword

When ten-year-old George Catlin's friend On-o-gong-way was brutally murdered, George learned that prejudice, mistrust, and hatred could bring tragic results. As an adult, he worked to bridge the gap between Indians and whites. He hoped that his paintings, books, exhibits, and lectures would help whites learn to see Indians as complex human beings, at a time when most white people associated Indians with massacres, thievery, and drunkenness or thought of them as "noble savages," uncorrupted by civilization.

"The North American Indian," George wrote, ". . . is an honest, hospitable, faithful, brave, warlike, cruel, revengeful, relentless—yet honorable, contemplative, and religious being."

In other words, not so different from anybody else.

But George couldn't save the Indians from the ravages of disease, alcohol, and war brought upon them by whites. In 1830, when he first went west, the fur trade and the government policies that supported it were already destroying the Indian cultures on the Great Plains. Buffalo, which the Indians depended on for food, clothing, and shelter, were being killed at a phenomenal rate. By the mid-1830s buffalo had replaced beaver as the most important commodity on the Plains, and some two hundred thousand buffalo skins a year were being exported from Indian country. For each buffalo skin, George wrote, white fur traders gave Indians a pint of whiskey. Over the next fifty years, an estimated sixty million buffalo would perish.

What he saw in the American West fueled George's passion for painting Indians. They were in trouble, and as a friend he felt that painting and writing about them was the best thing he could do to help. But he wasn't optimistic.

"They are *'doomed'* and must perish," he wrote, ". . . yet, phoenix-like, they may rise from the 'stain on a painter's palette,' and live again upon canvass [*sic*], and stand forth for centuries yet to come, the living monuments of a noble race."

This illustration from *Harper's Weekly* magazine shows men preparing buffalo hides for market. Behind the men on the left is a huge pile of buffalo bones.

Sketches in the Far West—Curing Hides and Bones. Engraving by Frenzeny & Tavernier, 1874. Library of Congress.

For all his fancy words, of course, George wasn't perfect. He had selfish reasons for painting Indians, too. In 1830 there were many portrait painters competing for business among the wealthy and powerful families of the East Coast. George thought that Indian portraits would be unusual and exotic and hoped that exhibiting them would be a more reliable way for him to make money and to earn respect as a painter. This turned out to be true, at least for a while.

Once George took his Indian Gallery to London and turned the exhibit into a razzle-dazzle show complete with singing and dancing, critics began to say he was exploiting the Indians for his own profit. Some felt that the live Indian shows in London and Paris were undignified. They accused George of providing cheap thrills for people who didn't really understand what they were seeing. Worse yet, he was accused of exaggerating his stories for theatrical effect, a charge that was probably true. His descriptions of the Mandan *O-kee-pa* rituals became more gruesome as he tried desperately to lure new audiences. Later, after the United States government published Henry Schoolcraft's book charging that the *O-kee-pa* didn't even exist, George's reputation never really recovered, at least not during his lifetime.

The success of the Indian Gallery made George popular, but he didn't know how to make that popularity last. He was a poor—or at least an unlucky—businessman and never made much profit. In fact, he was constantly scrambling to support his family. And though he loved his wife and children, his adventures took him away from them for months or years at a time.

In the end, after losing his family, George returned to the life he loved best—traveling, living off the land, exploring, and painting—for as long as he could. Then he retired to a solitary existence, paintbrush in hand, driven by the fervent hope that the value of his work would someday be recognized.

George Catlin was not the first to paint American Indians, but his

By the mid-nineteenth century most white people believed that American Indians were doomed to disappear, like the sun setting into the western sea. This painting expresses the idea that white domination of the continent was inevitable and that white civilization would soon extend all the way to the Pacific—an idea summed up in the term "Manifest Destiny."

Last of Their Race, by John Mix Stanley. Oil, 1857. Buffalo Bill Historical Center, Cody, Wyoming. Gertrude Vanderbilt Whitney Trust Fund Purchase; 5.75.

paintings and writings are the most complete record that exists of native American tribes, especially those of the Great Plains. By painting not only portraits but also landscapes, dwellings, dances, hunts, religious rituals, and the activities of daily life, he created precious images of Indian ways of life that have long since vanished. He captured on canvas the members of more than fifty tribes in North America alone, and countless more in South America.

Today George's paintings are treasured and appreciated both as works of art and as vivid depictions of the American past, even as his mixed motives are brought to light.

"There's no question . . . he was exploiting Indians and the West as a commodity," says W. Richard West, a member of the Cheyenne and Arapaho tribes and former director of the Smithsonian's National

Museum of the American Indian. "On the other hand, he was far ahead of his time in his empathy for Indians. Catlin swam against the tide to bring to light information about the Indians that depicts them accurately as worthy human beings and worthy cultures." West is particularly disturbed by the story of how George painted a dying buffalo.

A native person is challenged, I think, not to feel on some level a profound resentment toward Catlin. . . . I cannot imagine a Cheyenne, then or now, behaving this way toward a brother animal and, in particular, as a Plains Indian, toward a buffalo. . . .

But seen in the larger context of his time and place . . . he becomes far more appealing as being in many ways exceptional for his time. Whatever racist notions of the day may have been embedded in his imagination, Catlin placed great value on Indians and their cultures, revealing genuine concern at how they were being systematically stressed or destroyed by non-Indians.

Artist, explorer, showman, friend of the Indians—George Catlin's different roles sometimes clashed. He was a product of his time and shared its prejudices. His paintings and writings were popular in part because white people believed that American Indian cultures, languages, and peoples would soon disappear. But they have not disappeared, despite the assaults visited upon them by white civilization. Indian nations still fight for respect and justice. They strive to honor and preserve their traditions. And they continue to take pride in their ancestors, whose lives and spirit George captured so eloquently on paper and canvas.

George described many types of sacred dances among the Plains Indians, including a dance of thanksgiving for a good harvest, a prayer dance for hunting, and a dance celebrating the first snow in Autumn. This picture, based on a painting by Karl Bodmer, shows the leader of the Hidatsa Dog Society, Pehriska-Ruhpa, wearing the ceremonial costume of the Dog Dance. George painted an Eastern Sioux (Dakota) Dog Dance after seeing it performed at Fort Snelling in 1835.

PEHRISKA-RUHPA MÖNNITARRI KRIEGER IM AUZUGE DES HUNDETANZE. GUERRIER MONNITARI COSTUMÉ POUR LA DANSE DU CHIEN. MOENNITARRI WARRIOR IN THE COSTUME OF THE DOG DANSE [SIC]. AQUATINT AFTER AN ORIGINAL PAINTING BY KARL BODMER, BETWEEN 1839 AND 1841. LIBRARY OF CONGRESS

PEHRISKA-RUHPA.

Painters of the West

Although George Catlin was the only nineteenth-century painter to develop such a strong sympathy for the Indians and to speak out in defense of their ways of life, there were other artists who helped expose white Americans and Europeans to the peoples, cultures, and landscapes of the western frontier.

John Wesley Jarvis (1780–1840) traveled as far west as Ohio and as far south as Georgia to paint portraits, including one of Black Hawk. But most of his subjects were white. Unlike George, Jarvis was not interested in assembling a comprehensive collection of Indian portraits.

Charles Bird King (1785–1862) painted many Indians who visited Washington, D.C. He never traveled west himself.

Seth Eastman (1808–75), a captain in the U.S. Army, called himself a "soldier-artist." During the 1840s, while stationed at Fort Snelling in Minnesota, he painted Indians. His best work depicted scenes of Indian life and the surrounding landscape. Most of the illustrations in Henry Rowe Schoolcraft's book were based on Eastman's work.

The visit of Swiss artist Karl Bodmer (1809–93) to North America was brief. In 1833–34 he voyaged up the Missouri River with a scientific expedition. Afterward he returned to Europe and spent the rest of his life painting landscapes. (His first name is sometimes shown as Carl or Charles.)

In 1837 Alfred Jacob Miller (1810–74) traveled up the Platte and Missouri rivers and along what became known as the Oregon Trail. While doing so, he attended one of the last fur trappers' rendezvous. Miller spent most of his life painting western landscapes, Indian portraits, and scenes of wildlife based on sketches he made during this trip. Among the more unusual subjects he drew were an Indian woman throwing a lariat onto a horse, women riding in horseraces, and even a woman hunting buffalo.

John Mix Stanley's (1814–72) work was exhibited in the Smithsonian, but he failed, as George did, to convince the United States government to buy his collection. Tragically, most of his paintings were destroyed in the Smithsonian fire of 1865.

George Caleb Bingham (1811–79), Charles Deas (1818–67), and others entertained white audiences with scenes of the rough-and-tumble frontier.

By 1850 the artists of the so-called Hudson River School, following the lead of Thomas Cole (1801–48), had established pure landscape painting as the most popular genre. When Cole's friend Asher B. Durand (1796–1886) painted *Kindred Spirits* in 1849, it quickly became the most famous painting in America. Soon after, Frederic Church (1826–1900) created grand South American vistas that helped to secure his reputation as the leading landscape painter of the day.

Albert Bierstadt learned to paint mountain landscapes in Europe and applied his considerable technical skills to dazzling effect upon his return to the U.S. His romantic depictions of the Rocky Mountains, Sierra Nevada, and Pacific Northwest were very popular in the 1860s and 1870s.
SILVER LAKE, CALIFORNIA. ENGRAVING AFTER AN ORIGINAL PAINTING BY ALBERT BIERSTADT, CA. 1867. LIBRARY OF CONGRESS.

WHEN SIOUX AND BLACKFEET MET

Charles Russell worked as a ranch hand in Montana before devoting himself entirely to his art. He created more than two thousand paintings and sculptures depicting the West, including this imagined scene of a battle between Lakota Sioux and Blackfoot Indians.

WHEN SIOUX AND BLACKFEET MET, BY CHARLES M. RUSSELL. HALFTONE PHOTOMECHANICAL PRINT, 1902, CA. 1910. LIBRARY OF CONGRESS.

Albert Bierstadt (1830–1902) and Thomas Moran (1837–1926), with their depictions of the Rocky Mountains, the Sierra Nevada, the Yosemite Valley, and the Grand Canyon, inspired a nation that had been badly damaged by a brutal Civil War. Although George's dream of a national park in which Indians could live in their traditional ways never came to pass, the majestic wilderness captured by these and other landscape painters helped fuel the movement to establish the national-park system.

Later, artists such as Frederic Remington (1861–1909) and Charles M. Russell (1864–1926) contributed to the developing visual record of American Indians and the western way of life, as did photographer Edward S. Curtis (1868–1952). Today we have come to appreciate the work of Indian artists, past and present, such as the Hopi-Tewa potter Nampeyo (ca. 1860–1942) and the Salish painter Jaune Quick-to-See Smith (1940– , who have created their *own* images of Indian life and culture.

Ud-je-jock wears his peace medal,
eagle feathers, and face paint as
proudly as any adult.
UD-JE-JOCK, PELICAN, A BOY,
BY GEORGE CATLIN. OJIBWA. OIL, 1845.
SMITHSONIAN AMERICAN ART MUSEUM.
GIFT OF MRS. JOSEPH HARRISON, JR.

Author's Note

American Indians *or* Native Americans?

When Christopher Columbus sailed to North America, he thought he had landed in India, so he called the people who lived here "Indians." Today in the United States some native peoples prefer to be called "Native Americans," while others prefer the term "American Indians" or simply "Indians." In Canada, Indian tribes are more commonly called "First Nations." Throughout North and South America, those who lived here before the arrival of Europeans are also sometimes called "indigenous peoples," "aboriginal peoples," or "Amerindians."

Any person born in America is a "native" of America. And George Catlin is best known for his portraits of those who lived in what is now the United States, rather than those who lived in other parts of North and South America. Therefore, I have chosen to use the terms "Indians" and "American Indians" (rather than "Native Americans," "First Nations," or other terms) to refer to the people who lived in the Americas before the arrival of Europeans.

On the Words Squaw, Brave, *and* Warrior

The word *squaw* was derived hundreds of years ago from a word element that means "woman" in the Algonkian family of languages. Over time, whites began to refer to all North American Indian women as "squaws," and traders often used the word in a way that was very insulting. Eventually, the word developed an extremely negative association, and I have therefore avoided its use. I have also avoided the words *brave* and *warrior,* except when quoting George's letters, because they perpetuate the idea of American Indians as mythic beings or "noble savages," rather than real people.

Tribes, Chiefs, *and* Nations

When the Europeans came to the vast continents of North and South America, there were many different languages spoken among the Indians and many different political, social, and religious systems and beliefs. Not all Indians who spoke the same or similar languages or wore the same clothing necessarily thought of themselves as members of the same tribe. "Tribe" was a concept used by Europeans because it was easier for them to deal with Indians who fit neatly into groups. In reality, some Indians identified themselves as members of *clans;* others thought of themselves as belonging to certain *bands.* Today many Indians identify themselves by a clan or band name as well as a tribal name, and Indian tribes are often referred to as nations or tribal nations.

Likewise, in any one group of Indians, there was not necessarily one "chief." More often there were many chiefs—men with different political, religious, or other distinctions having to do with their achievements in hunting, warfare, and so on. White people, who came from European countries ruled by kings or queens, assumed that Indian cultures were organized in the same way, with one leader at the top. Because most whites did not understand or respect the Indians, they imposed their own idea of political structure by dividing Indians into distinct tribal groups, each having one chief. This was convenient for whites but could be disastrous for Indians. In treaty negotiations, for example, whites insisted on dealing with one "chief" who could speak for a whole "tribe," whether or not the Indians in question saw themselves as a tribe or acknowledged that chief's authority. This could lead to tragic misunderstandings.

Indian Names and Spellings

In George Catlin's time, few American Indians had a written language, and so he spelled names and words phonetically, the way they sounded. But he wasn't consistent—sometimes he spelled the same name several different ways. For example, Ha-wón-je-tah was also Ha-wan-ghee-ta and Ha-wan-je-tah.

In addition, sometimes an individual Indian had more than one name or used different names at different times in life. And a tribe—or a band, or a clan—might call itself by one name while English- or French-speaking trappers used another, with variations in spelling.

For all these reasons, figuring out how to spell Indian names and words can be quite a challenge. Spellings have changed over the years, and even today there is more than one accepted way to spell many Indian words, including the names of some tribes. For example, the word *tipi* can also be spelled *tepee* or *teepee,* but the first spelling is the most common. I have chosen to spell North American tribal names following suggestions made on www.native-languages.org, which is a website written by language experts, and by researching the websites of individual tribes. For South American tribes, I have consulted scores of websites and chosen the most common modern-day spellings. The website www.socioambiental.org/pib/indexenglish.htm, which is maintained by anthropologists, was particularly helpful.

For the names of individuals in this book, as well as for the *O-kee-pa* ceremony, I have used George Catlin's preferred spellings. Although George did not use accents to indicate emphasis in pronunciation, Catlin experts Thomas Donaldson, William H. Truettner, and George Gurney have done so, and I have followed their example.

Writing About American Indians

As a white person writing about American Indians, I have tried to be respectful of those whose cultural backgrounds differ from mine. But like George, I cannot completely erase my cultural biases, no matter how hard I try. Even with good intentions, it can be very difficult to see the world through the eyes of someone whose life experiences are radically different from one's own.

While writing this book, I discovered prejudices I didn't know I had, often based on romantic notions of American Indians that I learned from depictions in popular culture. Sometimes I found myself going back over what I had written and occasionally changing it to reflect a newfound awareness of the Indian point of view. My goal was to tell a story that children of all races and ethnic backgrounds could understand and enjoy.

George Catlin's Truth

In his books and letters, George did not recount his adventures in chronological order. During his lifetime this made it hard to verify where he went and when, and it hurt his reputation. George liked a good tale, and as a showman and yarn spinner he sometimes embroidered or exaggerated the truth. Scholars are still trying to sort out the routes he took in his travels, especially during the "lost years" of the 1850s. For example, Nancy Anderson, a curator at the National Gallery of Art who has done extensive research on the Cartoon Collection, is not convinced that George made it all the way to Siberia. Each historian and biographer makes her or his own assessment of George's truth, based on research and careful consideration of what is known and unknown. Where there is doubt or disagreement, I have used such phrases as "George recalled" and "according to George."

Timeline

1764	**Putnam Catlin, George's father, born April 5 in Litchfield, Connecticut.**
1770	**Mary "Polly" Sutton, George's mother, born September 30 in Pennsylvania's Wyoming Valley.**
1771	Benjamin West paints *Penn's Treaty with the Indians*.
1775	First shots of Revolutionary War fired in Lexington and Concord, Massachusetts.
1776	Declaration of Independence adopted, July 4.
1778	**Polly Sutton and her mother taken prisoner during Wyoming Massacre and later released.**
1783	Treaty of Paris signed, bringing end to Revolutionary War.
1786	Charles Willson Peale founds museum in Philadelphia.
1787	**Putnam Catlin moves to Wilkes-Barre, Pennsylvania, to practice law.**
	Constitutional Convention meets in Philadelphia.
1788	First Congress elected.
1789	**Putnam Catlin and Polly Sutton marry.**
	George Washington sworn in as first president of the United States.
1793	Eli Whitney invents the cotton gin, which revives slave economy.
1795	Gilbert Stuart paints portrait of president George Washington; he eventually paints more than a thousand portraits of prominent Americans.
1796	**George Catlin born in Wilkes-Barre, Pennsylvania, on July 26, the fifth of fourteen children.**
1800	Thomas Jefferson elected president.
ca. 1800	**Catlin family moves to farm in what would become Broome County, New York, near present-day Binghamton.**
1803	Louisiana Purchase.
1804–06	Lewis and Clark Expedition explores west of the Mississippi River.

1807	**Clara Bartlett Gregory born September 16.**
	Robert Fulton develops first commercially successful steamboat.
1808	Importation of slaves into the United States outlawed.
1810	**Catlin family moves to Hop Bottom, Pennsylvania.**
1811	Tecumseh (Shawnee) leads Indian Confederation against United States in Battle of Tippecanoe, Indiana Territory.
1812–14	War between United States and Great Britain.
1817	**Catlins move to Montrose, Pennsylvania.**
	George studies law in Litchfield, Connecticut.
1818	**George returns to Pennsylvania to practice law.**
1819–20	Writer Washington Irving publishes "Rip Van Winkle" and "The Legend of Sleepy Hollow."
1820	**George gives up law practice and moves to Philadelphia to become a painter.**
	Missouri Compromise maintains balance of free and slaveholding states.
1820–22	**George paints miniature portraits on ivory.**
1823	**George starts painting oils on canvas.**
	George sees delegation of Indians passing through Philadelphia.
	Monroe Doctrine declares the United States opposed to European colonization on the American continents.
1825	**George moves to New York City, is befriended by Colonel William Leete Stone.**
	George paints Erie Canal, completion of which encourages westward migration into Indian territories.
	President James Monroe proposes relocating all Indians beyond Mississippi River.
	Landscape painter Thomas Cole starts to make name for himself in New York.
1826	**George elected member of National Academy of Design, paints Sa-go-ye-wat-ha (Red Jacket) in Buffalo.**
	Growing religious revivalism leads to founding of American Temperance Society to discourage alcohol consumption.
	James Fenimore Cooper publishes *The Last of the Mohicans*, a novel that helps popularize idea that Indian contact with white civilization will cause Indians' extinction.
1828	**George exhibits twelve paintings at the American Academy of Fine Arts.**
	George marries Clara Gregory in Albany, New York, on May 10.
	George's brother Julius drowns in September.
	Andrew Jackson elected President.
1829–30	**George and Clara spend winter in Richmond, Virginia.**
1830	**George travels to St. Louis, meets General William Clark; travels with General Clark and begins to paint Plains Indians.**
	President Andrew Jackson signs Indian Removal Act, forcing thousands of Indians to resettle west of the Mississippi.
	Mormon Church founded.
1831	**George spends most of the year in the East, returns to St. Louis in December.**
	Nat Turner leads slave revolt.

1831	*The Liberator,* the first abolitionist newspaper, begins publication.
	Cyrus McCormick invents reaper.
1832	**George travels up the Missouri River on the *Yellowstone,* paints at Fort Pierre and Fort Union, then canoes down the Missouri, stopping to paint Mandans and Hidatsas.**
	George's letters published in Colonel Stone's New York newspapers.
	Surge of European immigrants begins to swell United States' population, strengthening economy and causing increased westward migration into Indian territories.
1833	**George travels with Clara to Pittsburgh, Cincinnati, Louisville, and New Orleans.**
	American Antislavery Society founded.
	Karl Bodmer travels up Missouri River, paints Mandans and other tribes.
1834	**George travels to present-day Arkansas and Texas with regiment of dragoons, rides back alone across prairie.**
1835	**George exhibits work in New Orleans, travels up Mississippi to Fort Snelling with Clara.**
	George exhibits work in Pittsburgh.
1836	**Clara gives birth to baby who dies at five days old.**
	George starts to prepare exhibit in Buffalo but abandons project and instead visits red pipestone quarry in present-day Minnesota.
	First missionaries, Marcus and Narcissa Whitman, arrive in present-day Oregon.
	Thomas Cole paints five-canvas *Course of Empire,* publishes essay on moral purpose of landscape painting.
	Essayist Ralph Waldo Emerson writes *Nature,* expressing a new American way to look at mankind's relationship to nature.
1837	**Indian Gallery opens in New York City in September.**
	Clara gives birth to daughter, Elizabeth (Libby), in December.
	Smallpox epidemic kills tens of thousands of Plains Indians.
	Telegraph patented by Samuel F. B. Morse.
	Painter Alfred Jacob Miller travels into Rocky Mountains.
1838	**Indian Gallery moves to Washington, D.C.; George tries to convince Congress to buy it.**
	Gallery moves to Baltimore, Philadelphia, and Boston.
	Cherokee Indians forced west—4,000 die on the "Trail of Tears."
	John James Audubon completes *The Birds of America,* 435 hand-colored engravings of 1,065 birds.
1839	**Indian Gallery reopens in New York and later in Philadelphia.**
	George sails for England, November 25.
	George and Clara's daughter Clara (Conny) born in December.
1840	**Official opening of London exhibit, February 1.**
	Clara and two daughters arrive in England in late June.
	Widespread enthusiasm for expansion of United States continues as westward migration grows.
1841	**George and Clara's third daughter, Louise Victoria, born in summer.**
	George publishes *Letters and Notes on the Manners, Customs, and Condition of the North American Indians.*

	Another Congressional resolution to buy Indian Gallery fails.
1842	Indian Gallery tours to Liverpool and other cities in Great Britain.
	Putnam Catlin dies, March 12.
1843	George and Clara's son, George, Jr., born in November.
	Ojibwas and Arthur Rankin arrive in London.
1844	Polly Sutton Catlin dies.
	North American Indian Portfolio published.
	George tours with Iowas—two Iowas die.
1845	Catlin family and Indian Gallery travel to Paris with Iowas; exhibit opens in June.
	Two more Iowas die; the rest go home.
	Clara Catlin dies in July.
	George hires Ojibwas, who perform for royal family.
	United States annexes Texas.
1846	Two Ojibwas die on tour; the others leave.
	George again appeals to Congress to buy Indian Gallery.
	George, Jr., dies.
	United States and Mexico declare war.
	Oregon Treaty establishes United States/Canada border.
1847	George starts paintings for King Louis Philippe.
	Congress rejects another proposal to buy Gallery.
	Frederick Douglass starts antislavery journal.
1848	George delivers paintings to Louis Philippe on eve of 1848 Revolution in France, flees to England with daughters.
	George publishes *Catlin's Notes of Eight Years' Travel and Residence in Europe.*
	Congressional committee votes to purchase Gallery for $50,000, but session ends without action.
	First Women's Rights Convention meets in Seneca Falls, New York.
	Mexican-American war ends; Mexico cedes vast territory to United States.
	Gold discovered in California.
1849	Senate debates buying Indian Gallery—approval fails by 2 votes.
	Asher B. Durand paints *Kindred Spirits.*
1850	George's financial hardship worsens.
	Novelist Nathaniel Hawthorne publishes *The Scarlet Letter.*
1851	Henry Schoolcraft publishes first volume of book on American Indians; later volumes accuse George of inventing many Indian stories.
	George goes deeper into debt.
	Isaac Merritt Singer patents sewing machine.
	Novelist Herman Melville publishes *Moby-Dick.*
1852	George, bankrupt, is thrown into jail; daughters taken to United States by Dudley Gregory.

1852   **Joseph Harrison pays George's debts and ships Gallery to Philadelphia.**
George returns to Paris.
Congress debates buying Gallery, but no action taken.
Novelist and abolitionist Harriet Beecher Stowe publishes *Uncle Tom's Cabin*.

1854   **George travels to South America and western North America.**
Writer/philosopher Henry David Thoreau publishes *Walden*.

1855   **Back in Europe, George meets with Baron Alexander von Humboldt, then returns to South America.**
Poet Walt Whitman publishes *Leaves of Grass*.

1857   **George returns to Europe, lives in Brussels, writes and publishes *Life Amongst the Indians*.**
Dred Scott decision declares Missouri Compromise unconstitutional—antislavery sentiment grows.
Frederic Church paints *Niagara*.

1858   **George may have revisited South America.**
Painter Albert Bierstadt travels west with survey expedition, later paints majestic landscapes of Rocky Mountains, Oregon, and California.

1859   Gold discovered near Pike's Peak, Colorado, and silver in Nevada's Comstock Lode.
Indians will subsequently lose more land to mining and cattle interests.
Frederic Church paints *Heart of the Andes*.

1860   **George lives in Brussels.**
Abraham Lincoln elected president of the U.S.

1861   **George publishes *The Breath of Life, or Mal-respiration*.**
Confederate states secede from Union, setting off Civil War.
Fighting between Indian tribes and U.S. continues during war.

1862   Passage of Homestead Act encourages settlement of Great Plains, leading to further loss of Indian land.

1863   Emancipation Proclamation frees slaves, January 1.

1864   Cheyenne and Arapaho massacred at Sand Creek, Colorado.

1865   President Lincoln assassinated.
Civil War ends; slavery outlawed by Thirteenth Amendment.

1865–77   Reconstruction.

1867   **George publishes *Last Rambles Amongst the Indians of the Rocky Mountains and the Andes* and *O-kee-pa*.**
United States buys Alaska from Russia.

1868   **George's youngest brother, Francis, visits him in Brussels.**

1869   Transcontinental railroad completed, May 10.

1870   **George publishes *The Lifted and Subsided Rocks of America*.**
George returns to United States, briefly opens exhibit in New York City.

1871   **Joseph Henry invites George to exhibit at Smithsonian.**

1872   **George becomes ill, moves into tower room.**
George dies in New Jersey, December 23.
Yellowstone National Park established.

	Congress purchases Thomas Moran's painting *Grand Canyon of the Yellowstone*.
1874–75	Red River War devastates southern Plains Indians.
1876	Indians, led by Sitting Bull, defeat General George Custer's troops at Battle of Little Bighorn, Montana.
1879	**Indian Gallery donated to Smithsonian by Joseph Harrison's widow, Sarah.**
	Few buffalo remain on Great Plains.
	Thomas Edison invents light bulb.
1886	Geronimo (Chiricahua Apache) surrenders, ending Indian wars in southwestern U.S.
1890	Last major armed conflict with Indians leads to massacre of Lakota Sioux at Wounded Knee, South Dakota.
1900	Indian population of North America reaches 200,000, its lowest number.
1909	**George's Cartoon Collection exhibited at American Museum of Natural History in New York City.**
1912	**American Museum of Natural History purchases Cartoon Collection from Elizabeth Catlin.**
1959	**Most of Cartoon Collection sold to Paul Mellon.**
1965	**Paul Mellon donates 351 Cartoon Collection paintings to National Gallery of Art in Washington, D.C.**
2000	Census puts Indian population of the United States at 4.1 million.
2004	Smithsonian opens new building for National Museum of the American Indian in Washington, D.C.

Notes

Full bibliographic information for titles cited here can be found in the Selected Bibliography, beginning on page 152.

PART 1: *First Steps on the Path, 1796–1830*

PAGE

2   "If he sees me": Catlin, *Life Amongst the Indians*, p. 25. Some scholars think George may have changed the details of this story or even made it up entirely. But George always maintained that it was true.

3   "These green fields": ibid., p. 32.

6   "the habit of writing": letter from Putnam Catlin to George Catlin, 1/21/1818. Roehm, *The Letters of George Catlin and His Family*, p. 19.

6   "study closely" and "girls & wine": letter from Charles Catlin to George Catlin, 11/27/1817. Ibid., p. 18.

6   "Another and stronger passion": Catlin, *Life Amongst the Indians*, p. v.

7   "My mind was continually reaching": Catlin, *Letters and Notes on the Manners, Customs, and Condition of the North American Indians*, vol. 1, p. 2.

8   "noble and dignified-looking": ibid. Some scholars think George didn't see this delegation of Indians until 1828.

12   "The history and customs": ibid.

13   "You will now be more happy": letter from Putnam Catlin to George Catlin, 5/30/1828. Roehm, p. 34.

| 16 | "What good man would prefer": Andrew Jackson's Second Annual Message to Congress, December 6, 1830. *Journal of the House of Representatives of the United States*, vol. 24, p. 26. |

PART 2: *The Frontier, 1830–37*

PAGE

24	"medicine painter": Catlin, *Letters and Notes*, vol. 2, p. 220.
24	"white chiefs": ibid., vol. 1, p. 226.
27	The story of Shón-ka and Mah-tó-che-ga is told in ibid., vol. 2, pp. 2–3 and 186–94.
29	"the big thunder canoe" and "big medicine canoe with eyes": ibid., vol. 1, p. 21.
30	"The Crows and Blackfeet": ibid., vol. 1, p. 42.
30	"sidelong looks": ibid., vol. 1, p. 29.
30	"black hair": ibid., vol. 1, p. 30.
31	"A boy, at the age of fourteen" and "He then returns home": ibid., vol. 1, pp. 36–37.
31	"cleanly in their persons": ibid., vol. 1, p. 23.
31	"the skins of snakes, and frogs": ibid., vol. 1, p. 40.
32	"The present chief" and "black and shining": ibid., vol. 1, pp. 49–50.
32–35	The buffalo hunt is described in ibid., vol. 1, pp. 24–28.
37	"at *sun-set*": ibid., vol. 2, p. 3.
39–40	The story of George's first encounter with the Mandans is told in ibid., vol. 1, pp. 105–11.
40	"grace and manly dignity" and "with the stillness of a statue": ibid., vol. 1, p. 145.
40–41	"procuring wood and water" and "the one who has the greatest": ibid., vol. 1, pp. 121, 118.
42	"the medicine cloth for sore eyes": ibid., vol. 2, p. 92.
42	"No part of the human race": ibid., vol. 1, p. 191.
42–43	"These people never bury": ibid., vol. 1, pp. 89–90.
43–44	"Each one's body" and "It was his duty": ibid., vol. 1, pp. 160, 161.
46	"We had heard the 'roaring'": ibid., vol. 2, p. 13.
47	"From its top": ibid., vol. 2, pp. 4–5.
47	"the skin of a black hawk": ibid., vol. 2, p. 211.
49	"great quantities of wampum": ibid., vol. 2, p. 41.
49	"ball-play dance": ibid., vol. 2, p. 125.

49   "ball-sticks": ibid., vol. 2, p. 125.
50   "tricks, and kicks" and "almost superhuman": ibid., vol. 2, p. 123.
51   "Hundreds are running together": ibid., vol. 2, p. 126.
51   "Sometimes for the distance": ibid., vol. 2, p. 77.
52   "The warrior's quiver": ibid., vol. 2, p. 56.
52   "They had every reason": ibid., vol. 2, p. 61.
53   "I have here represented him": ibid., vol. 2, p. 68.
54   "the most extraordinary horsemen": ibid., vol. 2, p. 66.
55–56   "One fine morning": ibid., vol. 2, pp. 88–89.
57   "decorated and ornamented": ibid., vol. 2, p. 139.
61   "'The white people'": ibid., vol. 2, p. 172.
61   "part of their flesh" and "a hole would be made": ibid., vol. 2, p. 166–67.
61   "We have heard": ibid., vol. 2, p. 173.

PART 3: *The Showman, 1837–54*

PAGE
64–65   "You can hardly imagine": letter from Putnam Catlin to Francis Catlin, 1/21/1838. Roehm, p. 126.
66   "This gallant fellow": Catlin, *Letters and Notes*, vol. 2, p. 220.
68   "settle down . . .": letter from Putnam Catlin to Francis Catlin, 7/12/1838. Roehm, p. 133.
68–69   "central, extravagant & fashionable": letter from George Catlin to Putnam and Polly Catlin, 1/10/1840. Ibid., p. 155.
70   "I am now in the midst" and "The suspense is painful": ibid., pp. 154–55.
71   "You will all rejoice": letter from George Catlin to Putnam and Polly Catlin, 2/17/1840. Ibid., pp. 156–57.
71   "When they arrive": letter from George Catlin to Putnam and Polly Catlin, 6/3/1840. Ibid., p. 171.
71   "with throbbing heart": letter from George Catlin to Putnam and Polly Catlin, 6/29/1840. Ibid., p. 172.
72   "We are here in a strange land": letter from Clara Catlin to Polly and Putnam Catlin, 10/29/1840. Ibid., p. 197.
73   "Our little daughters are fat and hearty": letter from Clara Catlin to Polly and Putnam Catlin, 2/28/1841. Ibid., p. 210.

73 "I would gladly retire": letter from George Catlin to Putnam Catlin, 6/19/1841. Ibid., p. 212.

76 "a low and contemptible fellow": letter from George Catlin to Clara Catlin, ca. January 1845, Archives of American Art, Smithsonian, roll 2136. Dippie, *Catlin and His Contemporaries*, p. 104.

80 "Every day that he afterwards": Catlin, *Catlin's Notes of Eight Years' Travels and Residence in Europe*, vol. 2, p. 272.

83 "Two idols of my heart": ibid., vol. 2, p. 324.

85 "sorrow and shame": letter from George Catlin to Daniel Webster, 4/15/1852. Dippie, p. 145.

86 "Catlin's splendid American Indian Collection": advertisement in the *Times* of London. Haberly, *Pursuit of the Horizon*, p. 178.

PART 4: *Wanderings, 1854–61*

PAGE

89 "With no other means": Catlin, *Last Rambles Amongst the Indians*, pp. 52–53.

90 "handsome dance": ibid., p. 224.

90 "*before* me during the day": ibid., p. 228.

90 "The songs of the day": ibid., p. 234.

90 "young rifle" and "very young": ibid. p. 249.

90–91 "'they had seen him every morning'": ibid., p. 252.

92 "no pen or pencil": ibid., pp. 305–6.

93 "wading . . . creeping and crawling" and "In the fresh air": Catlin, *Last Rambles*, pp. 59–64.

99 "wonderfully knitted": ibid., pp. 129–32.

99 "one of the party" and "I instantly recognized him": ibid., p. 155.

101 "the most powerful": ibid., p. 184.

101 "The rapidity": ibid., pp. 191–92.

103 "The firebrand fell": ibid., p. 198.

104 "If I were a younger man": letter from Alexander von Humboldt to George Catlin, 9/12/1855. Ibid., pp. 331–32.

107 "Nothing that ever was cooked": Catlin, *Last Rambles Amongst the Indians*, p. 222.

108 "almost extinguished": ibid., p. 279.

109 "Those that were near": ibid., pp. 283–84.

110   "Sometimes . . . cover hundreds of acres": ibid., p. 280.

PART 5: *Home at Last, 1861–72*

PAGE

111   "My dear, Sweet little Louise": letter from George Catlin to Louise Catlin, 4/22/1861. George Catlin papers, roll 2136, #637, Archives of American Art, Smithsonian, quoted in Christopher Mulvey, "George Catlin in Europe," in Gurney and Heyman, editors, *George Catlin and His Indian Gallery,* p. 78.

112   "I have had nothing": letter from George Catlin to Louise Catlin, 4/22/1861. George Catlin papers, roll 2136, #637, Archives of American Art, Smithsonian. Dippie, p. 357.

113–14   "quite robust and active": letter from General A. L. Chetlain to Thomas Donaldson, 6/22/1886. Donaldson, "The George Catlin Indian Gallery in the U.S. National Museum," pp. 715–16.

115   "is full of his anecdotes": from Francis Catlin's diary of his trip to Belgium, 11/21/1868. Roehm, p. 359.

115–16   "He must work": from Francis Catlin's diary of his trip to Belgium, 12/6/1868. Ibid., p. 369.

116   "until he finishes": from Francis Catlin's diary of his trip to Belgium, 11/23/1868. Ibid., p. 360.

117   "I don't know anything": letter from Richard Catlin to Francis Catlin, received 4/15/1870. Ibid., p. 401.

119   "In my old age": Haverstock, *Indian Gallery,* p. 216.

120   "Mr. Catlin," "not in an unhappy state," and "esteemed above anyone": letters from Joseph Henry to Dudley Gregory, 10/29/1872 and 10/31/1872. McCracken, *George Catlin and the Old Frontier,* p. 208.

121   "Oh, if I was down in the valley" and "What will become": Donaldson, p. 717.

121   "as an act of justice": *Annual Report, Smithsonian Institution, 1872,* pp. 436–38. Dippie, p. 432.

122–23   "There were about 450 paintings": Haberly, p. 228.

Afterword

125   "The North American Indian": Catlin, *Letters and Notes,* vol. 1, p. 8.

125–26 Statistics on the buffalo from the Smithsonian National Museum of the American Indian exhibit "George Catlin and His Indian Gallery," which toured the United States from September 6, 2002, to August 7, 2005.

126   "They are *'doomed'*": Catlin, *Letters and Notes,* vol. 1, p. 16.

128–29 "There's no question": Watson, "George Catlin's Obsession."

129   "A native person is challenged": W. Richard West's "Introduction." Gurney and Heyman, p. 21.

Color Illustrations

Mah-tó-he-ha, Old Bear, a Medicine Man, "on account of the art": Catlin, *Letters and Notes,* vol. 1, p. 36.
Big Bend on Upper Missouri, 1900 Miles Above St. Louis, "Scarcely anything in nature": ibid., vol. 1, pp. 74–75.

Selected Bibliography

BOOKS AND ARTICLES

Catlin, George. *Catlin's Notes of Eight Years' Travels and Residence in Europe, with His North American Indian Collection: With Anecdotes and Incidents of the Travels and Adventures of Three Different Parties of American Indians Whom He Introduced to the Courts of England, France, and Belgium.* London: Published by the author, 1848, 2 volumes.

———. *Last Rambles Amongst the Indians of the Rocky Mountains and the Andes.* London: Sampson Low, Son, & Marston, 1868.

———. *Letters and Notes on the Manners, Customs, and Condition of the North American Indians, Written During Eight Years' Travel Amongst the Wildest Tribes of Indians in North America (1832–1839).* London: Published by the author, 1841, 2 volumes.

———. *Life Amongst the Indians: A Book for Youth.* London: Sampson Low, Son, & Co., 1861.

De Voto, Bernard. *Across the Wide Missouri.* Boston: Houghton Mifflin, 1947.

Dillon, Richard H. *North American Indian Wars.* New York: Facts on File, 1983.

Dippie, Brian W. *Catlin and His Contemporaries: The Politics of Patronage.* Lincoln, Nebr.: University of Nebraska Press, 1990.

Donaldson, Thomas. "The George Catlin Indian Gallery in the U.S. National Museum (Smithsonian Institution) with Memoir and Statistics." *Annual Report of the Smithsonian Institution for 1885.* Washington, D.C.: Government Printing Office, 1886.

Ewers, John C. "George Catlin, Painter of Indians and the West," in *Annual Report of the Board of Regents of the Smithsonian Institution for 1955*. Washington, D.C.: Smithsonian Institution, 1956, 483–528.

Gurney, George, and Therese Thau Heyman, editors. *George Catlin and His Indian Gallery*. Washington, D.C.: Smithsonian American Art Museum, 2002.

Haberly, Loyd. *Pursuit of the Horizon: A Life of George Catlin, Painter and Recorder of the American Indian*. New York: Macmillan, 1948.

Halpin, Marjorie. *Catlin's Indian Gallery: The George Catlin Paintings in the United States National Museum*. Washington, D.C.: Smithsonian Institution Press, 1965.

Hassrick, Peter H. *The American West: Out of Myth, Into Reality*. Washington, D.C.: Trust for Museum Exhibitions in Association with the Mississippi Museum of Art, 2000.

Haverstock, Mary Sayre. *Indian Gallery: The Story of George Catlin*. New York: Four Winds Press, 1973.

McCracken, Harold. *George Catlin and the Old Frontier*. New York: Dial Press, 1959.

Moore, Robert J., Jr. *Native Americans: A Portrait. The Art and Travels of Charles Bird King, George Catlin, and Charles Bodmer*. New York: Stewart, Tabori and Chang, 1997.

Roehm, Marjorie Catlin, editor. *The Letters of George Catlin and His Family: A Chronicle of the American West*. Berkeley and Los Angeles: University of California Press, 1966.

Truettner, William H. *The Natural Man Observed: A Study of Catlin's Indian Gallery*. Washington, D.C.: Smithsonian Institution Press, 1979.

WEBSITES

George Catlin

"Campfire Stories with George Catlin: An Encounter with Two Cultures." The Smithsonian American Art Museum.
http://catlinclassroom.si.edu

"Catlin, George [1796–1872]: American Artist and Author" by Roderic A. Davis. Links to many George Catlin sites.
http://freepages.history.rootsweb.com/~dav4is/people/CATL121.htm

"George Catlin," by Donna Mann. National Gallery of Art.
http://www.ibiblio.org/nga/catlin.html

"George Catlin," by Theo Radic. Syuhktun Editions.
> http://www.angelfire.com/sk/syukhtun/catlin2.html

George Catlin's Indian Gallery. The Smithsonian National Museum of the American Indian.
> http://www.nmai.si.edu/exhibitions/catlin/index.htm

"George Catlin's Obsession," by Bruce Watson. *Smithsonian Magazine*, December 1, 2002.
> http://www.smithsonianmag.com/arts-culture/catlin.html

"George Catlin: The Medicine Painter." Virginia Museum of Fine Arts.
> http://www.vmfa.state.va.us/catlin/catlin.html

"The Magnificent Park of George Catlin," by Ronald E. Diener. April 1996.
> http://www.olympus.net/personal/buckley/Diener/Catlin.html

"Medicine Painter: George Catlin on the Upper Missouri, 1832," by Alice M. Cornell. University of Cincinnati Digital Press.
> http://www.ucdp.uc.edu/exhibits/catlin/catweb.html

The National Gallery of Art. 350 Catlin works created from the 1850s on.
> http://www.nga.gov/cgi-bin/psearch?Request=A&Person=4950

The Smithsonian American Art Museum. 627 works of art by Catlin from the 1830s.
> http://americanart.si.edu

Related Topics

American Indian Library Association.
> http://aila.library.sd.gov/

"The Black Hawk War of 1832," by James Lewis, Ph.D. Abraham Lincoln Historical Digitization Project.
> http://lincoln.lib.niu.edu/blackhawk/index.html

"A Century of Lawmaking for a New Nation: U.S. Congressional Documents and Debates, 1774–1875." *Journal of the House of Representatives of the United States,* vol. 24, p. 2. The Library of Congress.
> http://memory.loc.gov/cgi-bin/ampage?collId=llhj&fileName=024/llhj024.db&recNum=25

"Diaries, Narratives, and Letters of the Mountain Men." Library of Western Fur Trade Historical Source Documents. Links to primary-source documents, including the entire text of Catlin's *Letters and Notes.*
> http://www.xmission.com/~drudy/mtman/html/index.html

"A History of the Litchfield Law School." The Litchfield Historical Society.
> http://litchfieldhistoricalsociety.org/history/histlawschool.html

"Indian Removal Act: Primary Documents in American History." The Library of
     Congress.
     http://www.loc.gov/rr/program/bib/ourdocs/Indian.html
"Indigenous Peoples in Brazil." Instituto Socioambiental.
     http://www.socioambiental.org/pib/indexenglish.htm
"Kanza Cultural History." The Official Website of the Kaw Nation.
     http://www.kawnation.com/Culture/culthome.html
"A Little Basic Anthropology," by R. Edward Moore. Texas Indians.
     http://texasindians.com/cultanth.htm
"Native American Home Pages." Links to Native American sites, maintained by
     librarian Lisa Mitten.
     http://www.nativeculturelinks.com/indians.html
Oyate. Children's books about American Indians are discussed on this site.
     http://www.oyate.org/
"Preserving and Promoting American Indian Languages," by Laura Redish and
     Orrin Lewis. Native languages of the Americas.
     http://www.native-languages.org

INTERVIEWS

George Gurney, Chief Curator, Smithsonian American Art Museum. Interviewed
     5/19/2006.
Nancy Anderson, Curator of American and British Paintings, National Gallery of
     Art. Interviewed 5/19/2006.

PLACES TO VISIT

George Catlin's original Indian Gallery is in the Smithsonian American Art
Museum in Washington, D.C. The Cartoon Collection can be seen at the National
Gallery of Art, also in Washington. The New York Public Library in New York
City, the Newberry Library in Chicago, and the Yale Library of Western
Americana in New Haven, Connecticut, each have large collections of drawings.
Many other museums own art by George Catlin, including the Gilcrease Museum
in Tulsa, Oklahoma, the Denver (Colorado) Art Museum, and the National
Portrait Gallery in Washington, D.C.

Index